Is There an

Object

to Your Lesson?

Object Lessons for Teaching the Gospel

Richard R. Eubank

ISBN 1-890558-26-5

Published by

PUBLISHING & DISTRIBUTION L.L.C.
1-800-574-5779
Cover design by Tamara Ingram

Printed in the United States of America.
First printing: August 1998
Second printing: March 1999

This book is dedicated to my wife Mary
and to all those who love to teach the
gospel and who are anxiously engaged in
promoting the hope of a new tomorrow.

Table of Contents

Acknowledgements

I express great appreciation to Tyler Lawrence Kunzler, seminary teacher in Ogden, Utah, for willingly and enthusiastically contributing over half of the lessons used in this work.

With his permission, I have adapted them from two separate works: "Science Projects as Object Lessons," a paper written in 1996, and "Object Lessons Tied to Sections of the Doctrine and Covenants," a master's thesis written in 1997 at Weber State University in Ogden, Utah.

Also, a sincere thank you for the help of the following individuals without whose help this work would not have been completed in a timely and professional manner:

Editing and layout: Travis Anna Harvey

Cover design: Tamara Ingram

Lesson selection assistance: Stephen L. Adams, Dean H. Bowen, Kathy Coleman, Jackie Cook, Sharon Eubank, Eric Hansen, Jeff Lambson, Glenn Mitchell, Scott Randall, Robert H. Tippetts

Illustrations: Troy and Travis Anna Harvey

Title selection: Stephen L. Adams

Page quotations: Successories, Inc., all rights reserved, gave permission to use many of the marginal quotations.

Introduction

Several years ago I read that the Lord's method for teaching is to

1. Ask questions.
2. Tell stories.
3. Use parables.
4. Quote scripture.
5. Testify.
6. Draw out, not pour on.

I also once read the following list of questions for gospel teachers to ask themselves: What is it that my students need to learn? How will they relate the lesson to the gospel? Are they excited about the lesson or the gospel? Am I asking the Lord what and how to teach?

I believe that if we use the Lord's methods and ask ourselves these important questions, we will be more successful teachers of the gospel.

In Moses 6:63 it says that all things bear record of the Savior. We must be wise, selective, and prayerful, but basically any*thing* can be used in a lesson to relate a gospel truth. The Savior himself used wind, coins, animals, rocks, seeds and other common objects to teach the people in His day.

Object lessons can help involve students in the learning process, which will embed the concepts taught more firmly in their minds.

Object lessons take a specific, tangible object and relate it to an abstract concept. This helps the brain to connect ideas, thus increasing awareness, understanding, and retention.

This book contains object lesson ideas to help you present gospel topics in an interesting and eye-catching way that will help draw your students into a more in-depth discussion of important gospel principles. These object lessons are not meant to be complete discussions of any one topic. They are intended to be springboards into your own lessons. The objects are not the focus; the gospel principles you teach are.

Please expand and apply these lessons with your own inspiration, knowledge, and experience. When you teach them in your own words in your own way, the lessons will have more impact because of what you and your students bring to the lesson.

Decide which lessons are appropriate for your group, your lesson material, and the circumstances and adapt them accordingly. You might need to adapt the lesson for the age group you are teaching. You might want to combine lessons or parts of several lessons together to make your point. You might want to substitute a suggested object with a different one. Be creative.

Many objects can be used to teach several different gospel topics. Suggested gospel topics are given at the beginning of every lesson, but many times other topics could be taught as well. For example, one object discussed may be used to help teach faith, but you may see a way to use it to teach honesty.

The words "student" or "students" refer to any person or group of people you may be teaching, be it in Sunday School class, Family Home Evening, Seminary, Institute, Relief Society, Young Women, Priesthood, Primary class, etc. There are many opportunities to teach. These lessons can be adjusted to apply in many situations.

The scripture references at the bottom of each lesson are only a few suggested ones. Usually there is one each from the Old Testament, New Testament, Book of Mormon, and Doctrine and Covenants that in some way relates to the topics of each lesson. There are also some scriptures from the Pearl of Great Price included. Use your topical guide to find other scriptures that relate to the concept you are teaching.

Make this book your personal visual-aid idea storage book. Add new lesson ideas in the appendix as you think of new ways of using visual aids. Feel free to write in the book. Adding your personal input will make this a great resource for many years. And remember to share new ideas with friends.

Always practice an object lesson before you use it with your "class." And always strive to teach with the spirit.

May you find much enjoyment in these pages and many inspirational additions to your lessons.

This Cup

Topics

Atonement, Follow the Lord, Follow the prophet, Gratitude, Responsibility, Sacrament

Purpose

Students will better understand the various references to the word *cup* in the scriptures and think of the Savior more often.

Materials

✓ Enough clean square pieces of paper for each student (8.5" X 8.5" is good)

✓ Pitcher of water

Previous Preparation

Learn to fold the paper into a cup. Use the diagram to the right as a miniaturized template. In step 1, fold corner A to point A and corner B to point B.

Presentation

Show the students how to make a cup. Have them open their cups. Tell them that, like the cup, their minds should be open and willing to learn when they come to class. Read and discuss the following scriptures: Psalms 23:5; Matthew 26:39; Mark 10:38; 3 Nephi 11:11; Doctrine and Covenants 20:75. Ask the students if they think their cups will hold water. Pour water into their cups and have them drink. Relate the previous scriptures with their willingness to drink from the cup the Lord gives to each of us. Ask what it means to them to have their cups "runneth over."

Application

Assist the students in relating themselves to each of the scriptures used.

Scriptures

Psalms 23:5; Matthew 26:39; Mark 10:38; 3 Nephi 11:11; Doctrine and Covenants 20:75

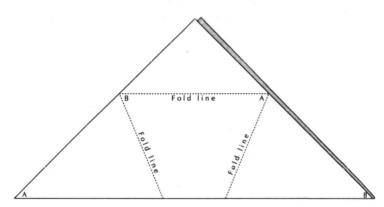

Step 1

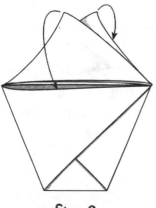

Step 2

Step 3

I Need Thee

Topics

Atonement, Christ

Purpose

The students will understand that no matter how hard they try, or how obedient they may be to the laws of the gospel, they cannot make it alone.

Materials

✓ A glass of water

✓ A large towel

Previous Preparation

Presentation

Spread the towel on the floor in the front of the class. Ask a volunteer to come up to the front and kneel down on both hands and knees on the towel. Make sure all can see what is happening. Place the glass of water on the back of the volunteer between the shoulder blades so the glass will balance by itself. Ask the student to remove the glass without spilling the water and place it on the floor in front of them.

Application

It is nearly impossible to complete the task of removing the glass without spilling a drop of water. The student must have help no matter how hard he or she tries alone. In the scriptures, the doctrine is taught that the law alone cannot bring salvation. There must be an atonement which God himself shall make. Mankind must have help.

Scriptures

Leviticus 17:11; Matthew 8:17; 1 Nephi 11:33; Mosiah 13:28; Doctrine and Covenants 19:16, 18

You can always tell when you are on the road of righteousness—it's uphill.

Life
in the Balance

Topics

Balance, Choices, Decisions, Faith, Obedience, Trust

Purpose

The students will understand how important it is to get their lives in balance with the gospel.

Materials

✓ A small piece of 3/8" plywood or pine

✓ A leather belt

Previous Preparation

Cut a balance hook from the 3/8" plywood or pine using the outline in step 1 to the right as a template.

Presentation

Show the balance hook. Ask the students what they think it is. Ask a volunteer to try to balance the small end on their pointer finger with the large end at the top so that the hook is upright. (The student most likely will not be able to do it.) Ask the volunteer to try balancing the hook horizontally off the end of their finger with the small end touching the finger and the large end hanging downward. (He will not be able to do it.) Ask the class if they think the volunteer would be able to do it if you added some weight to the large end. (They will probably think that is a crazy idea.) Tell them you think it will be easier to balance if you added weight to the large end. Ask how many believe you. Take the hook and place the leather part of the belt into the slot of the hook so that 2/3 of the belt hangs on one side as shown in step 2. Place the small end of the hook with the belt in it on the very end of the volunteer's finger and watch the look on everyone's face as it just hangs there magically. (The belt transfers the hook's center of gravity to directly under the tip of the finger.)

Application

Have the students turn to Matthew 6:32–33 and read aloud. What does this scripture suggest will help us keep proper balance in our lives? How is the gospel like this hook? (The hook could represent prayer and the belt could represent the needed weight of our accepting responsibility. The hook could also represent faith and the belt in this case could represent our works.) The gospel is a wonderful means to help us stay balanced in a very unbalanced world. However, we must believe in and use the gospel for it to work in our lives.

Scriptures

Job 31:6; Matthew 6:32–33; Alma 30:8; Doctrine and Covenants 132:8

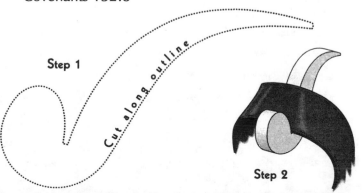

Step 1

Cut along outline

Step 2

People who don't cherish their elderly have forgotten whence they came and whither they go.

Many Are Called

4

Topics

Chosen of the Lord, Chastity

Purpose

The students will understand what the Lord means when He says "many are called but few are chosen."

Materials

✓ Five apples—three regular and two that have bites, holes, and dirt on them

✓ A chalkboard and chalk or large piece of paper and a marker

Previous Preparation

Prepare the two apples with the bites taken out of them.

Presentation

Place the five apples on a table and ask the class if they were allowed to select three of the apples to eat, which ones would they choose. (They will probably choose the clean ones.) Explain that the apples could represent people. Just like we choose which apples we would rather eat, the Lord chooses which people he wants to accomplish his work. On the chalkboard, create two columns, one titled "Chosen" and the other "Not Chosen." List personal qualities that might fall under each column. Then have the class name some individuals from the scriptures whose actions demonstrate these two sets of qualities (e.g., Adam, Isaiah, Sampson, Joseph Smith).

Application

Challenge the students to seek after the qualities of those who are classified as chosen. Ask them what the "defects in the apple" are in their lives. Which commandments are they having the most difficult time living? Encourage them to set goals designed to turn their weaknesses into strengths. Also point out and discuss that the "few who are chosen" are ones who have chosen the Lord and will do what He asks them to do.

Scriptures

Numbers 17:5; Revelation 17:14; Alma 13:3; Doctrine and Covenants 121:34

I couldn't wait for success, so I went ahead without it.

Written in Our Hearts

Topics

Christ Centered, Example, Righteousness

Purpose

The students will think about being more centered on Christ.

Materials

✓ An important document—birth certificate, marriage license, the Declaration of Independence, diploma, etc.—or a copy of one

✓ A blank piece of paper the same size

Previous Preparation

Presentation

Show the plain piece of paper and ask the students how valuable they think it is. Show them the document and ask how valuable it may be.

Application

Why is one piece of paper more valuable than the other? Point out that the main reason is because of what is written on them. Read together one or more of the scriptures below and discuss how Christ can be written in our hearts and what difference it would make to us and to others we come in contact with. Discuss how we can become more valuable to the Lord.

Scriptures

Proverbs 3:3; 2 Corinthians 3:3; Mosiah 5:12; Doctrine and Covenants 64:22

A real friend is a person who walks in when everyone else walks out.

Faithful or Slothful?

Topics

Church activity, Enduring to the end, Faithfulness, Obedience

Purpose

The students will see that they always need to be active in the Church and guard against becoming slothful. It is when we are slothful that we get into trouble and fall into temptation.

Materials

- ✓ A quart jar
- ✓ A racquetball, or other ball that will fit inside the jar
- ✓ A table top

Previous Preparation

Presentation

Place the ball on a desk and lower the mouth of the jar over it. Ask the students if it is possible to pick up the ball without any part of the jar mouth leaving the table. Have several students try. After they have tried, rotate the jar with the ball inside in a fast circular motion. Gradually increase the rotation speed until the ball climbs the sides of the jar. (It is lifted by the centrifugal force of its spinning.) You have lifted the ball off the table without the jar mouth being lifted.

While the ball is still spinning in the jar, lift the jar off the table while still rotating it. Stop rotating the jar in mid-air and the ball will drop to the floor.

Application

Just like the ball will ascend in the jar as long as the ball is moving, so will we stay firm in the gospel as long as we are moving forward and working towards eternal life. We, too, can be lifted up. However, once the forward movement is stopped, we will surely fall, just like the ball. Turn to Doctrine and Covenants 101 and discuss the following pattern.

vs. 47 Questioning (*What need hath my Lord of this tower?*)

vs. 48 Justifying (*Seeing this is a time of peace*)

vs. 50 Disobedience (*They became slothful and broke the commandments*)

When we follow this pattern, we too will cease to progress and will eventually fall. Discuss the pattern we should follow to remain strong and faithful.

Scriptures

Jeremiah 7:24; Hebrews 6:12; Alma 37:41; Doctrine and Covenants 101:46–54

Birds have bills, too, but they keep on singing.

Keep Them All

Topics

Commandments, Obedience, Temptations

Purpose

Students will understand that the more commandments they keep, the stronger they will be in resisting the temptations of the adversary.

Materials

✓ Twenty or so wooden popsicle sticks

✓ Marker

Previous Preparation

Write a different commandment on each stick (e.g., Word of Wisdom, Law of Chastity, Tithing, Pray, etc.).

Presentation

Take one of the sticks and hold it up. Ask a volunteer to come and read what is on it and then break it. (It will break easily.) Explain that if this were the only commandment you were keeping, it would be easy for Satan to overcome you. Read Doctrine and Covenants 42:29 and explain that the Lord has clearly asked us to live *all* his commandments. Put all the sticks together, reading a few as you do. Ask a volunteer to try to break them. (The student will not be able to.)

Application

This is a good lesson to help students see that they become stronger by keeping the commandments. You may want to hold up the broken stick and ask them which stick is their weak stick, or the commandment they are having the most difficult time living. Challenge them to keep all the commandments.

Scriptures

Leviticus 26:3–9; John 14:15; 1 Nephi 3:7; Doctrine and Covenants 42:29

Obstacles are what you see when you take your eyes off your goal.

Truth and Light

Topics

Commandments, Obedience, Truth and light

Purpose

Students will recognize the direct relationship between the number of commandments they keep and the truth and light they receive from the Lord.

Materials

✓ A lamp

✓ A flashlight

✓ A glow stick or clock with a glow dial

Previous Preparation

You may need to make the room as dark as possible by covering windows, etc.

Presentation

With all the lights on have the students read Isaiah 2:5. Turn out the lights and turn on a small lamp and have the students read Matthew 6:22. Turn off the lamp and turn on a flashlight and continuously move the beam around the room and have them read 2 Nephi 10:14. Now turn off the flashlight and activate the glow stick and ask the students to read Doctrine and Covenants

93:26–29. Put away the glow stick and have them try reading anything.

Application

It is more difficult to receive the word of God as the light of truth dims, or our keeping the commandments diminishes. Help the students understand that it is easier to do their work and receive truth when they have all the lights on, or are keeping the commandments. Once we start breaking commandments, then the light gets darker and darker until we are lost completely. Challenge them to think of one or two of their life's darker areas and to set goals to make them brighter.

Scriptures

Isaiah 2:5; Matthew 6:22; 2 Nephi 10:14; Doctrine and Covenants 93:26–29

First the thought within one's head, next the word will soon be said, then the deed you'll see instead.

Draw Upon Your Experience

Topics

Communication, Patience, Testimony, Understanding

Purpose

The students will begin to understand how difficult it can be to explain something to others so that they can picture it for themselves. They will better appreciate good communication and have more patience.

Materials

✓ A brown paper sack

✓ An object with an interesting shape

✓ Paper and pencil for each student

Previous Preparation

Place the object into the paper sack. The students should not see the object.

Presentation

Give each student paper and a pencil. Inform them that they are to draw the object found in the paper sack. They will not be able to look at it or feel it. There will be one person who will, without lifting out the object or looking into the sack, describe the object by feeling its shape so all can draw it correctly. This student should not name the object.

After one person has tried to describe the object, have a second person come forward and, under the same rules, proceed to help the class complete the drawing. After the students feel they have the object drawn, show them the object and compare it with their drawings.

Application

From this experience, one develops an appreciation for being able to communicate well. It is not easy to describe an object you cannot see. Sometimes it is even difficult to describe what we *do* see. Mormon wrote that it was nearly impossible to describe the blood and carnage that he witnessed. Students should now have a better understanding of how Mormon felt. Encourage the class to practice patience with others and with themselves as they learn to communicate well.

Scriptures

Joshua 18:1–8; Colossians 4:6; Mormon 4:11; Doctrine and Covenants 88:78

When nobody around you seems to measure up, check your yardstick.

Treat or Deceit?
(Part One)

Topics

Deceit, World

Purpose

Students will understand that the world offers enticing and beautiful gifts that are really of little value and are disappointing in comparison to the Lord's gifts which are of real value.

Materials

✓ A plain, drab package with the scriptures inside

✓ A beautifully wrapped package with dirt inside

Previous Preparation

Prepare both packages.

Presentation

This is part one of a two-part object lesson and the second part should be presented within a week or so of this part. While each lesson teaches a different principle, they work better being taught one after the other.

Show the two packages and ask the students if they saw both under the Christmas tree, which they would choose. Which would most people choose? (The beautiful one.) Have two students come up and each open a package so all can see the contents.

Application

Discuss how the world often masks worldly filth in enticing packages. Compare how some things in the gospel are incredibly valuable but may not at first appear exciting.

Scriptures

Proverbs 11:18; Matthew 13:22; 1 Nephi 16:38; Doctrine and Covenants 89:4

What lies behind us and what lies before us are tiny matters compared to what lies within us.

Ask and Unmask
(Part Two)

Topics

Personal revelation, Prayer, God's gifts

Purpose

Students will realize the importance and wonderful blessing of asking Heavenly Father for direction.

Materials

✓ A drab package with dirt inside

✓ A beautifully wrapped package with a treat inside (cookies, candy, etc.)

Previous Preparation

Prepare the packages and arrange with one of the students to raise his hand at a given time during the presentation and ask you what is in the packages.

Presentation

This is part two of a two-part object lesson. Part one (Lesson 10) should be presented first.

Show the two packages and ask the students what they learned from the last lesson. Which package would they choose? (They will probably choose the drab package.) At this point, have the student who is helping with the lesson ask you what is in both packages. Have the student come up front so you can whisper the true contents in the student's ear. Then have the student sit down without saying anything. Ask the students again how many would choose the drab package and how many would choose the beautiful one? (The student who knows the true contents will choose the beautiful one.) Tell them they may have the contents of whichever package they choose. Take another vote. (They will probably choose the pretty package this time.) Have two students come forward and open the packages.

Application

Give the contents of the beautiful package to those who chose it. Ask those who first chose the drab package but later changed to the beautiful one why they changed their minds. (Most likely because they trusted the student who asked you about the contents.) Discuss the importance of asking Heavenly Father for wisdom in making decisions. We should ask him for the gift of discernment. Our personal testimonies and the gift of the Holy Ghost will also direct us for good. We should also rely on our faith in the prophet and our leaders. Sometimes the Lord blesses us with wonderful things that seem too wonderful to be true. We need his help as we learn to make wise choices.

Scriptures

Daniel 2:22; 1 Corinthians 2:10; Moroni 10:4–5; Doctrine and Covenants 46:8

You'll always miss 100% of the shots you don't take.

Rope Magic

Topics

Deceit, Satan, Miracles, Knowledge

Purpose

The students will understand how we can be deceived by the tricks of Satan.

Materials

✓ A vase, detergent jug, bleach bottle, or some similar opaque container

✓ A piece of soft rope about two feet long

✓ A rubber ball that will just fit inside the opening of the jug

Previous Preparation

Practice the presentation ahead of time.

Presentation

Pass around the rope and the vase for the students' inspection. Tell them you have magic glue in the bottom of the vase that can stick and unstick on command. Just before you put the end of the rope into the vase, put in the rubber ball without letting anyone see you. Wind the tail of the rope around the neck of the vase and turn the whole thing upside down. The rope will fall but not come out. The rope and the ball cannot both come out at the same time, so it appears to be glued in the vase. If the wedge is tight enough, the tail of the rope can be unwound from the neck of the vase and swung back and forth without coming lose. To release the rope, just push it back into the vase when in an upright position. The ball will fall into the vase and the rope will come out.

Application

Is this magic? (No.) How does Satan try to deceive us? Give examples in advertising, movies, television, the Internet, etc. Do Satan and his followers often give us part truths which make their lies seem right? What part does ignorance play in deception? Discuss how we can make sure we are not deceived.

Scriptures

Daniel 1:20; Acts 16:16; Alma 1:32; Doctrine and Covenants 28:11; 46:7

Bubbling Over with Desire

Topics

Desire, Obedience, Spirit, Work

Purpose

The students will understand how important it is to possess the desire to do good.

Materials

- ✓ A clear glass
- ✓ Water
- ✓ Liquid dish soap
- ✓ A tray
- ✓ Dry ice

Previous Preparation

Make a solution of soap and water and pour it into the clear glass.

Presentation

Put the glass of soapy water in the middle of the tray so all can see. Tell the students that unless there is something added to the water, it will remain there doing essentially nothing but evaporating into the air. It will continue to do so until it is gone. Drop the small piece of dry ice into the glass and watch the bubbles come up and over the top of the glass. The bubbles may even fill your tray if enough soap and ice are used.

Application

The glass of soapy water represents our lives. The bubbles represent the expansion and growth of our souls. The dry ice represents a desire to do good and do well at doing good. It also represents the Spirit that gives us the strength to move forward toward exaltation. One must have the Spirit or the desire to perform the work of a Latter-day Saint. Relate the story to what made Nephi different from his rebellious brothers, or any other story of a similar nature.

Scriptures

Proverbs 10:24; 1 Corinthians 14:1; Alma 32:27; Doctrine and Covenants 4:3

Keep your face to the sunshine and you cannot see the shadows.

String of Time

Topics

Eternity, Obedience, Time, Stewardship, Plan of salvation, Choices

Purpose

The students will have a better perspective of earthly time and the importance of our time in mortality.

Materials

✓ A string long enough to reach across the room

✓ A bead

Previous Preparation

Thread the string through the bead so the bead is in the middle of the string.

Presentation

Stretch the string with the bead in the middle across the full length of the room. Attach the ends to the wall or have two students hold the ends. (This could be done before class.)

Application

Ask the students what they think the bead represents. (This world, mortal time) What does the string on either side of the bead represent? (One side represents our pre-mortal existence and the other side represents the life after this.) Does it really matter what we do on this little, tiny world? Are there some on the premortal side who made unwise choices? (Satan and his followers chose to reject this progressive, mortal experience.) Who determines how far we progress on the post-mortal side? (We do.) Read and discuss several scriptures and help the students to understand the importance of the time they have today.

Scriptures

Psalms 90:2; 2 Corinthians 4:18; Alma 34:33; Doctrine and Covenants 38:1; 52:13; 60:13; 72:3

Don't wait for your ship to come in... swim out to it.

Salty Enough?

Topics

Example, Obedience, Salt of the earth

Purpose

The students will understand how important it is to live up to the covenants of the gospel and to be "saviors." They will also learn what the Lord meant when he said that "ye are the salt of the earth" and what salt is "that has lost its savor."

Materials

✓ Two transparent salt shakers
✓ Pure salt
✓ Sand and a dark spice

Previous Preparation

Fill the two salt shakers, one with pure salt and the other with a mixture of salt, sand, and the dark spice.

Presentation

Ask the students what several uses for salt are. (Preservation, flavoring, water softening, melting ice, antiseptic, etc.) Ask which salt shaker they would pick to flavor their food. (They will probably choose the clean salt.) Ask why they would not want the salt mixed with sand and spices. Explain that the salt in that shaker has lost its pure qualities and is no longer useful for its intended purpose.

Application

Read several of the scriptures below (as well as other applicable ones) and ask the students to relate the scriptures to themselves. (If salt has lost its savor or tasteful quality, it is then good for nothing.) Ask them to think about what type of salt they are. Help them see that by keeping the commandments they can be the salt that the Lord can use to preserve their lives and to help save others.

Scriptures

Isaiah 42:6; Matthew 5:13; 3 Nephi 12:13; Doctrine and Covenants 101:39–40; 103:9–10

No one can predict to what heights you can soar. Even you will not know until you spread your wings.

What Do You Expect?

Topics

Expectations, Change, Potential, Deceit, Sin

Purpose

Students will understand how their expectations change when they permit things to change their potential.

Materials

✓ A raw egg

✓ Food coloring

✓ Hypodermic needle (see your local pharmacy)

✓ A clear bowl

Previous Preparation

Color the inside of the egg by injecting it with a hypodermic needle full of food coloring.

Presentation

Show the egg. Put it into the clear bowl. Ask the students to tell you everything they know about an egg. Describe an egg. What is the egg's potential? What are its uses? What would you expect to find inside an egg? How do you know all this about an egg? Crack open the egg into the bowl and watch the students' reaction.

Application

What changed the egg's contents? We are born as special children of God. Why do we sometimes fall short of our potential? What do we sometimes let enter into our lives that keeps us from reaching our potential?

"All the water in all the world, no matter how hard it tried, could never sink the smallest ship, unless it got inside.

And all the evil in all the world, the blackest kind of sin, could never hurt you the least little bit unless you let it in."

Author unknown

Scriptures

Psalms 119:11; Proverbs 21:4; 2 Peter 2:14; 2 Nephi 4:27; 9:49; Doctrine and Covenants 10:25–26

The best way to predict the future is to create it.

A Grain of Wheat to Help Us Eat

Topics

Faith, Trust

Purpose

The students will be encouraged to exercise more faith.

Materials

✓ A grain of wheat

Previous Preparation

Presentation

Conceal the grain of wheat in your hand and explain to the students that you have something in your hand that could feed a hundred people. Ask them if they trust you. Have them guess what it could be. Show them the grain and ask how it could feed a hundred people. Explain that if we plant this grain, it will grow into a stalk of wheat bearing about fifty other grains of wheat. If we plant those fifty, we will produce 2500 other grains. Planting those will yield 125,000. Plant those and we get 6,250,000 grains of wheat, enough to feed over a hundred people. All this in only four plantings.

Application

Do we have faith in what the Lord tells us, or what the prophet tells us, even if our vision is not broad enough to see the purpose? What does it take to have faith? Why did the Lord use a grain of mustard seed to symbolize faith? Is faith a gift from God? If we practice obedience will that gift of faith come to us? What can we do this week to increase our opportunities for receiving that gift?

Scriptures

Psalms 118:8; Luke 17:6; Alma 32:28–43; Doctrine and Covenants 26:2

A bend in the road is not the end of the road... unless you fail to make the turn.

Big Bad Balloon

18

Topics

Fear, Faith, Confidence

Purpose

The students will realize that most fears have little substance and that through faith and confidence we can overcome fear.

Materials

✓ A large balloon

✓ Marker

✓ Pin

Previous Preparation

Blow up the balloon without tying it and write FEAR on it in large letters with the marker. Let out the air.

Presentation

Begin blowing up the balloon, making sure the students see the word fear. Ask for examples of different fears we sometimes have. Blow up the balloon fully and discuss how big it is. Ask the students if they had several of these in the front seat of a car, would it hinder driving? If they had several tied around their neck, would it hinder daily activities? Discuss the problems the balloons would cause and ask for solutions. Offer a tiny but powerful solution. (A pin.) Pop the balloon and point out how little substance there really is to fear (the remains of the balloon) compared to a moment ago (when fully blown up). What is the difference? (Just air.)

Application

Discuss the fact that our fears are mostly air, not much real substance, even though they can sometimes look and seem overwhelming. Discuss what the pin could represent. (Scriptures, positive self talk, faith in our potential as children of God, remembering and concentrating on the things we can do and not past failures, etc.)

Scriptures

2 Kings 6:16; 2 Timothy 1:7; Moroni 8:16; Doctrine and Covenants 38:30

You cannot discover new oceans unless you have the courage to lose sight of the shore.

Wrapped in Safety

Topics

Follow the Prophet, Atonement, Obedience, Faith

Purpose

Students will understand that following the Prophet will keep them safe from the world.

Materials

✓ A wool blanket

Previous Preparation

Presentation

What if the Prophet told us there was a deadly sickness coming and, to be safe, we were to sleep for the next little while covered by a wool blanket? Show the blanket. (In this example, the wool could represent a lamb, the Lamb of God; the blanket could represent being wrapped in righteousness.) What would you say? Possible reactions:

1. Too hot. 2. Why? 3. Don't have a wool blanket. 4. Can't afford one. 5. My friends will hear about it and laugh at me. 6. I'll use my comforter instead. 7. Can I just keep it in my room?

Read the story in Exodus where the Israelites were instructed to put the blood of a lamb on their door posts.

Application

The Children of Israel were told to put the blood of a lamb (representing the atonement) on their door posts. Why? Some of their responses could have been

1. I don't have a lamb. 2. Would a goat do? 3. What will my neighbors think? 4. Too messy. 5. What if I just keep my lamb tied up in the front yard?

Compare these commandments to other commandments the Lord asks us to do. What might some of our responses be? What should they be?

Scriptures

Exodus 12:7; John 10:27; Jacob 6:8; Doctrine and Covenants 20:26

Some people dream of worthy accomplishments, while others stay awake and do them.

Healing the Hurt

Topic

Forgiveness

Purpose

Students will understand that forgiving others is a self-healing process.

Materials

✓ A board

✓ A large nail

✓ A hammer

Previous Preparation

Presentation

Show the board to the students and explain that it represents each one of them. Ask for several examples of being hurt by others. Drive the nail into the board without allowing the point to go through the other side. (Leave enough of the nail head showing to be able to pull it out.) Explain that the nail represents the hurt. Explain that the people who hurt us may or may not know that they hurt us. They may care or not care that they hurt us. They may even move away, out of our lives. But should we live our lives with the nail sticking into us like this? (Carrying the hurt.) What do we need to do? (Pull it out.) What is that called? (Forgiveness.)

Pull out the nail. The nail is out but there is still a hole in the board. How can we fix that? (Wood putty, sandpaper, and maybe paint.) How can we fix our lives? (Once we really forgive, the Lord will do the healing so there are no scars.) Turn the board over and show how it would look when repaired properly.

Application

Help the students understand that even though it is sometimes very difficult to forgive, it is in their best interest to do so, and that the Lord will help in the process.

Scriptures

Isaiah 1:18; Matthew 6:15; Mosiah 26:31; Doctrine and Covenants 64:7–11

There are many things in life that will catch your eye, but only a few will catch your heart... pursue those.

Please Take Note

Topics

Forgiveness, Repentance

Purpose

Students will learn to seek forgiveness for something they have done wrong, or to forgive someone who has done them wrong.

Materials

✓ A notepad of self-adhesive notes

Previous Preparation

Presentation

Read Doctrine and Covenants 64:7–14 and discuss it. Discuss what repentance is and how to repent. Hand each student a self-adhesive note. Have each of them think of a situation in their lives in which they either need to seek forgiveness from another person or need to forgive another for something that brought them sorrow. Have the students briefly describe this situation on their notes. Remind them that this description is confidential and that no one is going to see what they are writing. Once each student has written a situation on a note, have them stick the notes in the scriptures in Doctrine and Covenants 64 so that one edge or corner sticks out when the book is closed.

Application

Suggest that the students keep the note in their scriptures until they have either taken the steps to be forgiven or to forgive another. Once they have carried out this process, they should then take out the papers and discard them. The note will remind them to apply in their own lives the lesson they have learned. You may wish to use fluorescent colored notes so they stand out as a daily reminder to the students of what they need to accomplish.

Scriptures

Isaiah 1:18; Matthew 6:15; Mosiah 26:31; Doctrine and Covenants 64:7–14

We make a living by what we get; we make a life by what we give.

Keep the Lid On

Topics

Genealogy, Family history, Sealing powers

Purpose

Students will understand that when the scriptures say "And he shall turn... the heart of the children to their fathers," the Lord is making reference to the promised sealing powers to be restored by Elijah to the Prophet Joseph Smith in the Kirtland Temple.

Materials

✓ A quart jar with lid

✓ A toy man, woman, and child, or paper cutouts of each small enough to fit into the jar

Previous Preparation

Presentation

Take the family figures and place them in the jar without the lid in place. Shake the jar around and up and down until some of the figures fly out of the jar. Put the figures back in the jar but this time screw on the lid. Again shake the jar. Explain that the meaning of the word "turn" as used in the scriptures means to seal or bind. This could be compared to turning the lid on the jar.

Application

Students should be able to see the difference between the two examples. Discuss the importance of the sealing powers in the temple and doing temple work for the dead. Because work for the dead is only possible on earth, our hearts must be turned to our fathers. Open up the discussion to the sealing of living parents and children and ask what the shaking of the jar represented. What does the lid on the jar symbolize? Why is being sealed a strength in keeping your family together? What are some of the activities you and your family can become involved in to make the lid a little tighter?

Scriptures

Malachi 4:5–6; Matthew 16:19; Helaman 10:7; Doctrine and Covenants 2:2

In life what sometimes appears to be the end is really a new beginning.

The Meek Will Seek

Topics

Gifts of the Spirit

Purpose

Students will understand that each one of them was given a gift of the Spirit when they were baptized and confirmed a member of the Church. They will understand that there are many more gifts of the Spirit they can receive if they seek after them.

Materials

✓ Three gift-wrapped boxes, a small, medium and a large one, each with a more or less uninteresting object inside—perhaps a wrench, a cup, a magazine, or a stapler

Previous Preparation

Prepare the gifts as described.

Presentation

Have a volunteer come to the front of the room and inform the students that they may have their choice of one of the three gifts but that the volunteer will get to make the final choice. Ask the class which box they think the volunteer should choose, and then let the student make the final choice. Before the student opens the box, tell the class that each of them has been given a gift from the Lord. Ask the students to turn to Doctrine and Covenants 46 to find out what you mean. Have them search in this section to see if there are any of the gifts they feel they have been blessed with. Have the volunteer open the chosen gift to see what it is.

Application

Ask the students what they think of the gift. Ask them how they would feel if they received the gift on their birthdays. Explain that at some point in time the gift could be very useful. They might not see the need for its use now, but later on it may be much needed. Gifts of the Spirit need to be sought after when they are needed, much like the student chose a gift. We may not understand how to use them right away, but we will someday find them very useful. Challenge the students to think of what gift would help them the most in life right now, and then to earnestly pray and seek for that gift.

Scriptures

Exodus 31:3; 1 Corinthians 7:7; Mormon 9:7–8; Doctrine and Covenants 46

Yesterday is but a dream. Tomorrow a vision of hope. Look to this day, for it is life.

Lay Aside and Abide

Topics

Gospel, Scriptures, Spirituality, World

Purpose

Students will see the importance of putting spiritual needs before the needs of the world.

Materials

✓ A $20 bill

✓ An empty box

✓ A sign reading, YOUR TESTIMONY

Previous Preparation

Place the sign in the box so it cannot be seen and put the box on a desk or table in the front of the room.

Presentation

Call on one of the students to come up and say that you are going to give the student a choice between what is in the box or $20. If the student chooses the $20, then show him or her what is in the box and ask if the $20 is the final choice. Ask the class what is more important in life—having money or having a testimony.

Application

Read together Doctrine and Covenants 25:10. You may wish to ask the class how this object lesson relates to laying aside the things of this world (the love of money, etc.) and seeking for the things of a better (a testimony, the scriptures, the gospel, etc.). To help them see how much they value their testimonies, ask them how much they are worth. Would anybody sell theirs for $50, $100, $1000, $10,000, or not at all? Then lead them into a discussion of what the "things of this world" are and what the "things of eternity" are. Help them to understand how to place more value on eternally important things.

Scriptures

Psalms 119:2; Matthew 6:33; Jacob 2:18; Doctrine and Covenants 25:10

A mind once stretched by a new idea never regains its original dimensions.

We Mean to Be Clean

Topics

Gospel, World, Handling worldly things

Purpose

Students will understand that we have to live in and work in a world that has much wickedness, but we do not have to be of the world to do so.

Materials

- ✓ A tray
- ✓ Garbage or dirt
- ✓ Rubber gloves

Previous Preparation

Put the garbage or dirt on the tray.

Presentation

Explain that we must live and work in a world that has much wickedness. Show the garbage or dirt. Put on the gloves and begin rummaging or working in the garbage or dirt as you talk. Explain that many times we cannot avoid coming in contact with "the evils of the world." Some activities or occupations we may be involved in may require us to have more contact with worldliness than others. Ask what can keep us from being influenced by or having the evils of the world rub off on us. Direct the answers toward gospel principles, such as keeping the Sabbath holy, studying and pondering the scriptures, paying an honest tithe, praying every day, etc. When you are through, remove the soiled gloves and shake hands with several students thanking them for their comments.

Application

The students will understand how keeping gospel principles (or wearing gloves) keeps us clean from the evils of the world.

Scriptures

Isaiah 1:16; James 1:27; Alma 60:23; Doctrine and Covenants 59:9

Soft or Hard?

Topics

Gospel centered, Christ centered, Faith

Purpose

The students will think about the nature of their hearts and commit to be more gospel oriented.

Materials

- ✓ A fresh egg
- ✓ A hard boiled egg

Previous Preparation

Hard boil one of the eggs.

Presentation

Have a volunteer come up and spin each of the eggs. Ask the students what the difference is. (The fresh egg won't spin very well; the hard boiled egg spins easily.) Tell them one has a center that has become hardened and the other has a soft heart. Ask if they can tell which is which.

Application

Compare our hearts to the eggs. If our hearts are hardened, what will our lives be like? (We will spin around in circles and probably fall.) If our hearts are soft, what kind of character do we have and what kind of lives do we live? (Teachable.) Do you ever feel like your life is going around in circles? What can you do to stabilize your life? (Practice being more Christ centered.) Discuss examples of people the students know who they believe are Christ centered.

Scriptures

Proverbs 23:7; Ephesians 4:14; 1 Nephi 12:17; Doctrine and Covenants 29:7

You become successful the moment you start moving toward a worthwhile goal.

Eye Care

Topics

Gospel principles, Holy Ghost, Iron rod

Purpose

Students will realize that they must always live the principles of the gospel. They must never close their eyes to the light of the gospel or they will fall.

Materials

Previous Preparation

Presentation

Have the students balance on one foot. Then have them balance on one foot and tilt their heads back. Finally, have them balance on one foot, tilt their heads back, and close their eyes. (They will lose their balance.)

Application

Sometimes we are asked to go through difficult times in life. We must never close our eyes to gospel principles or we will fall. Always look toward the light. With the light of the gospel and the gift of the Holy Ghost, we should not be, nor need we ever be, in the dark. Even though some things are difficult, we will not fall if we keep our eyes focused on the light.

Scriptures

2 Kings 6:15–20; Matthew 6:22; 3 Nephi 10:12–13; Doctrine and Covenants 50:25

Blow Up

Topics

Gospel wisdom, World, Fulfilling life's mission

Purpose

Students will better understand what their potential is and how to fulfill it.

Materials

- ✓ A balloon
- ✓ A pop bottle
- ✓ A drinking straw

Previous Preparation

Practice the presentation.

Presentation

Have a student blow up the balloon and let the air out again. Now stuff the end of the balloon in the pop bottle so just the hole end is sticking out. Have the student attempt to blow up the balloon again. (It cannot be done. As the balloon expands in the neck of the bottle, air is trapped within the bottle. For the air inside the balloon to expand, the trapped air must escape.) Place a straw inside the bottle along the side of the balloon so the air can escape. Now have the student try to blow up the balloon again. (It can be done.)

Application

Make the following comparisons: the balloon is our potential to be fulfilled; the bottle is the world, gospel ignorance, sin, etc.; and the straw is gospel wisdom, a conduit of prayer, etc. We, as Latter-day Saints, are taught how to reach our full potential. When we live the gospel's true principles, we will succeed. You may want to point out that our full potential (the fully blown-up balloon) can only take place after we leave this world (the bottle) and continue on into the next. The Lord's plan is for us to become like him, and do the things he does.

Scriptures

Daniel 4:27; Matthew 3:15; Alma 37:35; Doctrine and Covenants 131:6

Accept challenges so that you may feel the exhilaration of victory.

Let Them Shout, Filter Out

Topics

Holy Ghost, Still small voice, Listening

Purpose

Students will identify those distractions that deter them from listening to the voice of the Spirit. They will understand how to use the Holy Spirit as a guide so that they are not deceived.

Materials

✓ A chalkboard or poster board

✓ A piece of chalk or marker

✓ A blindfold

Previous Preparation

Presentation

Choose two students to come up in front of the room and blindfold one of them. Draw a small circle on the chalkboard and tell the blindfolded student all he or she has to do is mark an X in the circle while the other person stands in the back of the room giving directions. However, the rest of the class can yell out other directions and make it difficult to hear. Have the students try out the exercise.

Application

Students will understand better what it means to take the Holy Spirit as their guide. Discuss what sort of things are distractions to the Spirit. What does the yelling class relate to in your life? Are there people trying to lead you astray? Likewise, are you trying to lead your friends astray? Students will discover several analogies on their own as to how this lesson relates to their lives.

Scriptures

Proverbs 3:6; Ephesians 4:14; Mosiah 26:6; Doctrine and Covenants 101:16

Your attitude almost always determines your altitude in life.

Pinpoint the Solution

Topics

Holy Ghost, Spirit, Listening

Purpose

Students will understand that they need to listen carefully in order to hear the whisperings of the still small voice.

Materials

✓ A small sewing needle or a pin

Previous Preparation

Presentation

Tell the students that you want to conduct a little experiment. You are going to drop a pin on the desk and would like everyone to be quiet so they can all hear it. Drop the pin and have all the students who heard it raise their hands. Repeat the experiment until each has a chance to hear the pin drop.

Application

This experiment can be compared to how one can hear the whisperings of the still small voice. Ask why the Spirit is often described in this way. Why do they think it is also described at the same time as being something that pierces to the center and causes your bones to quake? Explain that the Spirit whispers so that only those who are listening can hear it. Do your daily surroundings make it easier or more difficult to hear the Spirit of the Lord?

Scriptures

1 Kings 19:12; Mark 4:24; 1 Nephi 17:45; Doctrine and Covenants 85:6; 101:16

To be a winner, all you need to give is all you have.

The Treasure

Topics

Joseph Smith, Bible, Scriptures

Purpose

Students will better understand the importance of the work Joseph Smith was performing in translating the Bible.

Materials

✓ A homemade treasure map

✓ Treats

Previous Preparation

Prepare the treasure map and hide somewhere in the room the treats that are the "treasure."

Presentation

Display a copy of your treasure map and ask the students if they would be willing to take the time to follow the map if they knew there was treasure to be found at the end. (Instead of a treasure map, a diagram of your room could be used, with the objective being to find a treat you have previously hidden.) Next hold up a set of scriptures and explain that they are like the map, only they do not lead to earthly riches but to eternal life, which is the greatest treasure of all. Ask them if they would be willing to listen to and follow the instructions in the scriptures like they are willing to follow a treasure map. Have them follow the map and find the treat.

Application

Afterwards, ask several questions for discussion. Why did you follow the directions on the diagram? Why did you take the time to study it instead of just looking around the room? Explain to the students the importance of reading the scriptures to gain direction in their lives. Discuss the importance of Joseph Smith's translating the Bible. Read several passages from the Bible and the same passages from the Joseph Smith Translation and compare them. Discuss how important to our understanding Joseph Smith's "treasure" is.

Scriptures

Deuteronomy 6:6–7; Acts 17:11; Mosiah1:3–4; Doctrine and Covenants 73:3–6

In the middle of every difficulty lies opportunity.

Write On

32

Topics

Journal

Purpose

Students will realize the importance of keeping a journal.

Materials

✓ A book by a well-known author, easily recognized by the students

✓ A journal

Previous Preparation

Presentation

Show the well-known book and tell the students the name of the author. Ask them what it means to be a famous author? How many books does a person have to write to be an important author? Hold up a journal. (Make sure the students can tell what it is.) Ask again how many books a person must write to be an important author. (Just one, your journal.)

Application

Discuss the importance of keeping journals.

Scriptures

Malachi 3:16; 1 Nephi 1:1; Doctrine and Covenants 85:9; Abraham 1:31

Keep your head and your heart in the right direction and you'll never have to worry about your feet.

A Bad Egg?

Topics

Judging, Knowledge, Understanding, Wisdom

Purpose

Students will see that it is important not to make hasty judgements of others. We usually do not have enough information or knowledge.

Materials

✓ Two raw eggs

✓ A clear bowl

Previous Preparation

Make a small hole in each end of one of the eggs and blow out the inside. Make the other dirty and unappealing on the outside.

Presentation

Show both eggs and ask the students to choose which one they would like to eat. (They will most likely choose the clean one.) Ask them why they chose that one. Discuss the differences of the two eggs (appearance) and how they think each one might taste. Hold up the clean one and then crush it in your hand. Then break open the dirty one into the bowl, showing the clean, good inside. Ask the students what they learned.

Application

How do you look at other people—your peers, strangers, neighbors, family members? Discuss the fact that we presume too much to think we can accurately judge others merely by their appearance or by first impressions. The Lord judges us by our hearts.

Scriptures

Leviticus 19:15; John 7:24; Mormon 8:20; Doctrine and Covenants 11:12

Some succeed because they are destined to, but most succeed because they are determined to.

The First One

Topics

Judging, Sin, Forgiveness, Repentance

Purpose

The students will understand that all have sinned and are unable to judge righteously without the Lord's help.

Materials

✓ A large stone with the words "the first one" written on it

Previous Preparation

Prepare the stone.

Presentation

Place the stone before the students. Ask what the Lord said about casting the first stone. Read John 8:1–11. How could seeing this stone on your dresser or nightstand every morning help you?

Application

Encourage students to avoid the pernicious sin of judging others. Leave the stone in a visible area for a week or so as a reminder of this lesson. Or, make a stone like it for each of the students to take home.

Scriptures

Leviticus 19:15; John 8:1–11; Mosiah 29:12; Doctrine and Covenants 10:37; 18:10

Patience carries a lot of wait.

Yearn to Learn

Topics

Knowledge, Wisdom

Purpose

Students will understand that the Lord is pleased when we take the time to diligently study fields that relate to secular knowledge that can also apply spiritually. We are to seek wisdom from various fields of study.

Materials

✓ An assortment of college text books or library books from some of the following fields of study: astronomy, geology, history, economics, politics, and geography

Previous Preparation

Presentation

One by one hold up some of the books and ask the students why they think it would be important to study this sort of information. Read Doctrine and Covenants 88:77–80, 118. Why did the Lord say that he wants us to study such things as these (vs. 80)? He wants us to be prepared to magnify the callings that may come our way.

Application

Ask students what field of study interests them the most from the books you have brought. Then inquire as to how that study could help them if they were called to serve a mission. Encourage them to be well rounded by studying and developing a broad background in various subject areas. You may wish to explain that a college education includes a number of classes in general studies.

Scriptures

2 Peter 1:5; Alma 30:44; Doctrine and Covenants 88:77–80, 118; Moses 6:63

You must have long-range goals to keep you from being frustrated by short-range failure.

Lighten Up

Topics

Light, Example, Christ, Guidance, Darkness

Purpose

The students will understand how the Lord is the "light" of the world, and how they should be guided by that light.

Materials

✓ Dark paper to cover windows and door seams

✓ The lights in your room

Previous Preparation

Cover the windows and other areas of the room to make it as dark as possible.

Presentation

Ask the students how we see with our eyes. Step to the light switch and turn off the lights making it as dark as possible. Point out that even though we can see with our eyes, there are times when our vision is limited. Turn on the lights and read John 8:12 and ask how the demonstration relates to this scripture. (In both instances light is necessary.)

Application

Ask the students to read John 8:12 again. Explain that Jesus often demonstrated great truths by associating them with symbols people were familiar with. For example, when speaking with the woman at the well Jesus talked of living water. As lamp stands in the temple gave forth light at the feast of tabernacles, Jesus revealed himself saying, "I am the light of the world." For those who grow in faith and testimony and follow Christ, there will be no darkness. They will forever be guided by the "light of the world."

Scriptures

Isaiah 2:5; John 8:12; Acts 13:47; Helaman 13:29; Doctrine and Covenants 6:21

The loftier your goals, the higher your risk, the greater your glory.

It's a Trap

Topics

Listening, Holy Ghost, Obedience, Follow the prophet

Purpose

Students will understand that it is not always easy to listen to and follow the voice of the Lord and the voice of His servants. Students will see that there are many influences that draw them away from following the counsel of church leaders.

Materials

- ✓ A mouse trap
- ✓ A pencil
- ✓ A blindfold
- ✓ A one-dollar bill, piece of candy, or other "prize"

Previous Preparation

Presentation

Demonstrate how the mousetrap works. Set it, then show how it can break a pencil when triggered. Blindfold a student and say that you have set the mousetrap and are now placing a dollar on it. All the student has to do to get the dollar is to listen to one person in class who will be giving directions as to how close he is to the trap. Place the trap on the desk. Take the blindfolded student out of the room. Come back and instruct the others to try to distract the individual from hearing the directions from the student telling the truth. Bring the student back in to try to get the dollar. When the student is unable to understand and follow the directions given by the "true guide," it will be impossible to get the dollar without harm. (Of course, allow the student to come close to the trap but without endangering him or herself.)

Application

Ask who the blindfolded student represents. (Each of us.) Who does the student giving directions represent? (The voice of the Lord or His servants.) How about the distractions? (Those things that hamper us from following our church leaders.) What did the trap represent? (The temptations we sometimes fall into from not listening to what we are warned about.) How could you better understand the voice of the Lord and His servants? What are the distractions in your life that make it difficult to follow the Lord's direction? What are the traps that you are falling into in your life? What are some ways to avoid falling into them?

Scriptures

1 Kings 18:21; John 10:27; 1 Nephi 22:20; Doctrine and Covenants 1:14

The sky is the limit when your heart is in it.

Draw the Right Conclusion

Topics

Listening, Listen to the Spirit, Communication

Purpose

Students will understand the importance of listening and communicating and that listening to the Spirit is a skill that needs to be developed.

Materials

✓ Paper for each student

✓ Pens or pencils for each student

Previous Preparation

Presentation

Have a student come up and, without lifting the pencil off the paper, draw a simple unfamiliar pattern without letting the others see it. (Not just a triangle or a circle.) Then have the student describe the pattern to the others and have them draw it based on the verbal description. Have the students compare their drawings and discuss where the communication was unclear.

Application

It is important for students to learn to give clear directions, and for them to listen carefully to the Spirit, and to other good teachers and guides.

Scriptures

Proverbs 29:18; Luke 11:28; Alma 5:46; Doctrine and Covenants 20:26

When the day is over and you have done your best, wait the results in peace.

Cannot Live Without It

Topics

Living water, Christ, Gospel

Purpose

The students will see by demonstration and experience how important having the gospel of Jesus Christ is to spiritual life.

Materials

✓ A cup

✓ A pitcher of water

✓ A small potted plant

Previous Preparation

Presentation

Have a student come to the front of the room. Give the student the empty cup. Fill it with water and have the student water the plant with half the water and drink the rest.

Application

Ask the students what the chief value of water is in our lives. (It helps sustain life.) When man looks for life on other planets, what one substance do we look for to know life exists there? (Water.) Jesus and the Samaritan woman were at the well to get a drink to quench their thirst. Jesus chose a most appropriate symbol to teach her—water. Water is life, especially to people in an arid climate like that of Palestine. Without water, vegetation and human life die. Point out that the woman, like hot, thirsty land without water, was spiritually dead. She needed the living water of the gospel in her life to restore her spiritual life. We need that living water in order to really live.

Scriptures

Jeremiah 2:13; John 4:5–30, 39–42; Alma 5:34; Doctrine and Covenants 10:66

Use what talents you possess. The woods would be very quiet if no birds sang there except those that sang best.

That's My Rock

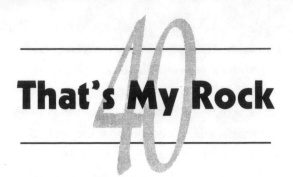

Topics

The Lord knows us individually, Trust in the Lord

Purpose

Students will understand that God really does know each and every one of us personally.

Materials

✓ Enough rocks of about the same size so that there is one for each student

✓ Several blindfolds

Previous Preparation

Presentation

Give each student a rock. All the students should carefully observe and feel their rocks. Have them write their initials on their rocks so they can be identified later. Gather up the rocks. Invite several students up to the front and blindfold them. Place the pile of rocks in front of the first student. This student should feel each rock until his or her own is found, pass the rest to the next person, and so on. After all the students have found their own rocks, discuss their methods for identifying their rocks.

Application

Read together John 10:27 and ask who the sheep are. (Us.) How does the Lord know us? (We lived together for a long time in our pre-mortal existence; the Lord is God, He knows everything and everyone.) How can we trust Him with our secrets and problems, our joys and sorrows? (He descended below them all; He knows all feelings and He knows all the answers; He loves us unconditionally and has only our good in mind.)

Scriptures

Psalms 95:7; John 10:27; 1 Nephi 22:25; Doctrine and Covenants 121:24

It takes both rain and sunshine to make a rainbow.

It's a Miracle

Topics

Miracles, Faith

Purpose

The students will understand the power the Lord has and the impact that power must have had on those who witnessed it on earth in his day.

Materials

✓ Clear household ammonia

✓ Water

✓ A pitcher made of dark glass or stone for water

✓ A clear jar, large enough to hold the contents of the three goblets

✓ White vinegar

✓ Three clear goblets

✓ An eyedropper

✓ Approximately 5 milliliters of phenolphthalein (A school chemistry department will have this.)

✓ Alcohol (ethyl or rubbing)

✓ One small container

Previous Preparation

Mix two tablespoons of ammonia with 24 ounces of water in the pitcher. In the clear glass jar put a small amount of vinegar, just enough to cover the bottom of the jar. In the small container, add fifteen drops of phenolphthalein to six ounces of alcohol with the eyedropper. Put ten drops of the phenolphthalein-alcohol solution in each goblet. This solution will evaporate quickly so do this just before the miracle demonstration.

Presentation

Pour the water-ammonia solution into the goblets with the phenolphthalein-alcohol solution. As this solution fills the glass, it mixes with the alcohol solution and turns red. It looks like water is turning to wine. You can change the "wine" back to water by emptying the goblets of wine into the glass jar with vinegar in it.

Discuss the Lord's omnipotence. Do we have miracles today? What is the purpose of miracles?

Application

This demonstration is easy to perform and very effective. Your students may never forget this experience. Discuss Jesus' miracles.

Scriptures

Exodus 7:9; John 2:1–11; 2 Nephi 26:13; Doctrine and Covenants 45:8

Do not follow where the path may lead. Go instead where there is no path and leave a trail.

Can You Light It?

Topics

Miracles, Prayer, Power, Faith

Purpose

The students will better understand the power of the Lord through experience and demonstration. They will also understand that prayers are answered.

Materials

✓ A tissue

✓ Pie tin

✓ A table

✓ Paper matches

✓ A glass of water

Previous Preparation

Presentation

Wad the tissue into a ball and put it in the pie tin on the table in front of the students so all can see. Have a student come to the front of the room. Instruct the student to burn the tissue paper by lighting it with the paper matches. Give the student the matches. Just before the match is struck, stop the student and explain that this is too easy. Take the glass of water and pour it on the tissue in the pie tin, leaving just a corner of the tissue dry so it can still be lit. Have the student continue with the task. Just before the match is struck a second time, stop the process and explain that it is still too easy. Now take the match book away so there is no strike pad to light the match.

Application

Have the students turn to 1 Kings 18:18–39 and read the account of Elijah the prophet and the priests of Baal. Discuss the miracle and the power of prayer and faith.

Scriptures

1 Kings 18:18–39; Acts 3:6; 1 Nephi 17:48, 52; Doctrine and Covenants 45:8

There is no exercise better for the heart than reaching out and lifting people up.

Direction Connection

Topics

Patriarchal blessings

Purpose

Students will better understand and appreciate the direction they can receive from their patriarchal blessings.

Materials

✓ A blindfold

✓ A compass

Previous Preparation

Presentation

Have a student come to the front of the room and ask which direction is north. (Most students will know.) Now blindfold the student and spin him or her around several times. With the blindfold still in place, again ask which way is north. (The student probably will not be able to point in the right direction.) Remove the blindfold and have the student sit down again. Now show the students a compass and ask how it helps in finding directions.

Application

Just like the compass gives direction when you are lost, a patriarchal blessing does the same thing. Many times we think we know what direction our life is taking (like the student first knew what direction was north). However, sometimes in life we become confused and are left to wonder if we are on the right course (like when the student was blindfolded). The compass/patriarchal blessing gives us the needed direction. It helps us get on the right track and then helps us stay there. Have students share examples of how having their patriarchal blessings have helped them (without sharing sacred, personal examples of the blessings' contents). Encourage those students who have not yet received their patriarchal blessings to consider doing so.

Scriptures

Genesis 48:14–15; John 16:13; 1 Nephi 16:10,16; Doctrine and Covenants 124:91–93

The future belongs to those who believe in the beauty of their dreams.

Tied to Your Choices

Topics

Peer pressure, Wisdom, Agency

Purpose

Students will see that they do not have to be led around
by others doing things they really don't want to do.

Materials

✓ A long rope or string

Previous Preparation

Presentation

Bring several students close together and wrap the rope
or string loosely around them so they can still move but
they are bound together. Now have them play "follow
the leader" with you around the room doing various
things that are difficult to do being tied into a group—
things like follow you around chairs, under tables, over
obstacles, hopping on one foot, etc.

Application

Ask if the experience was difficult. Ask them why they
stayed in a tied-up bundle? You never said they had to
stay as a group. That was their choice. They could have

gotten out of the string. Would the tasks have been easier outside the string?

What is peer pressure? Why should we make our own wise choices in life? Why should we choose friends who uplift us and not those who don't support our ideals and standards?

Scriptures

Joshua 24:15; Ephesians 4:14; Mormon 5:18; Doctrine and Covenants 53:2

If it is to be, it is up to me.

A Map in Your Lap

Topics

Plan of salvation

Purpose

Students will see the importance of the gift of the Lord's plan of salvation.

Materials

✓ A treasure map

✓ A graphic depiction of the plan of salvation

Previous Preparation

Make a treasure map. You could draw it on parchment paper, crumple it up and burn the edges to give it a more "authentic" appearance. Also make the plan-of-salvation map.

Presentation

Show the treasure map and ask why it is so important to follow it exactly. Show the plan-of-salvation map and ask the same question.

Application

Ask how the two maps are the same and how they are different. Explain that we ultimately choose the "treasure" we want in life, either worldly treasures or the Lord's treasures. The final decision lies with us.

Scriptures

1 Corinthians 15:22; 2 Nephi 9:13; Moses 6:62; Abraham 3:22–23

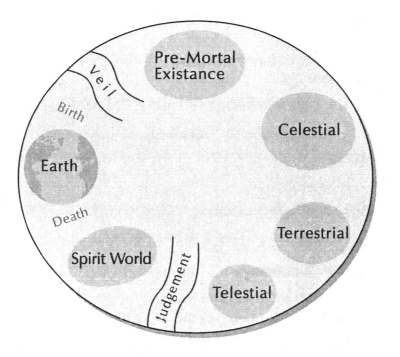

The only limitation is your imagination.

Plan for Man

Topics

Plan of salvation

Purpose

The students will better understand the wonderful plan Heavenly Father has designed for us.

Materials

- ✓ A poster board
- ✓ A self-adhesive note
- ✓ Questions pertaining to the plan of salvation

Previous Preparation

Draw on the poster board a representation of the plan of salvation. Prepare a series of questions pertaining to the plan of salvation. Cut the self-adhesive note into the shape of a person.

Presentation

Stick the person-shaped note at the beginning of the plan of salvation. This person represents each of the students in the class. Explain to the students that the object is to reach the celestial kingdom. In order to progress and move forward, we all must be tested and proven. Tell them they will need to answer various questions concerning their pre-mortal life, this life, and the life to come. Ask the students a series of questions that relate to the plan of salvation. With every right answer, move the figure forward a step. The students may discuss the questions amongst themselves before they give you their answers. The students must be unanimous in their answers.

Application

Using the board in a game-like way makes learning fun. Participation is very high and the students must think about each question which helps them remember what is being taught. They will recognize the importance of progression and learning in the plan of salvation.

Scriptures

Ezekiel 37:12; Revelation 12:7; Ether 12:19; Doctrine and Covenants 76

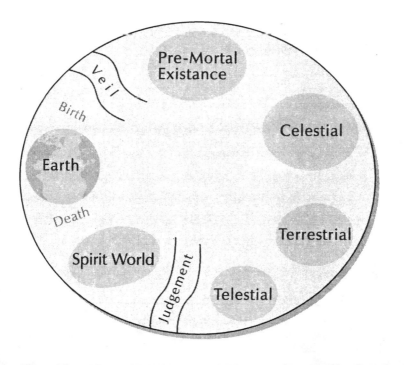

Shake It Up

47

Topics

Power, Creation

Purpose

The students will understand that the world was created by a divine creator and not by chance.

Materials

- ✓ A clear plastic bag
- ✓ Connecting blocks, or parts of any device that can be put together

Previous Preparation

Presentation

Place all the connecting blocks in the plastic bag. Have a student come forward and take the bag. Tell the student to assemble the blocks into an automobile or other object that the pieces create, but to do this only by shaking the bag. The student may not arrange the blocks in any other way other than to shake the bag.

Application

Ask the students if it is possible to assemble the blocks in the bag by just shaking them. Just by chance could the pieces fall into the right place? What are the odds of such a thing happening?

As in the example above, all the elements were present before the earth was created. What were the odds of all the elements falling together in the right order and beginning to function? Discuss how wonderful and kind the Lord is to use his power to bless our lives. The Lord created our earth, our solar system, and the universe. They have order and purpose.

Scriptures

Genesis 1–2; John 1:3; 2 Nephi 11:7; Moses 2–3

A warm smile thaws an icy stare.

Unthinkable

Topics

Power, Creation, Christ's power

Purpose

The students will better understand the vastness of the Lord's creations and the power he possesses for our benefit.

Materials

✓ A medium-sized container of clean sand

✓ A tray

Previous Preparation

Presentation

Put some sand onto the tray and have several or all of the students press a finger into the sand. Ask them to count the particles of sand that stick to their fingers. Have them guess how many particles are in the container. Ask them to imagine trying to count the particles of sand along the western coast of Alaska to the tip of South America and back up the eastern side to Greenland. Have them turn to Moses 7:30 and read together. Remember, the earth is not even the beginning of the Lord's creations.

Application

Ask the students why the Lord has created all these worlds. Then have them turn to Moses 1:39 and read why. If the Lord is doing all this for us, and has all this power, surely he has the power to forgive our sins and help us through life. Now turn to Matthew 11:28–30 and read together. Discuss what a yoke is and why the Lord's yoke is easy. (A yoke is a harness for joining together a pair of oxen, usually consisting of a cross-piece with two bow-shaped pieces, each enclosing the head of the animal. See Webster's Dictionary.)

Scriptures

Jeremiah 51:15; Matthew 11:28–30; Colossians 1:16; Doctrine and Covenants 76:24; Moses 1:39; 7:30

Failure is only the opportunity to more intelligently begin again.

With Just a Finger

49

Topics

Personal power, Self-discipline, Knowledge

Purpose

Students will realize that with just a little knowledge, a little faith, and a little self-discipline, we have great power and can overcome great obstacles.

Materials

✓ A chair

Previous Preparation

Presentation

Have a large, male student sit in the chair in front of the rest of the students and tilt his head back a little. Ask a small, female student to come up and place her forefinger on the other student's forehead. Tell her that with her finger she is not to allow his head to move forward. Ask the sitting student to stand up. He will not be able to unless his head moves forward so that his center of gravity is located over his feet. Have another student come up to the front and keep you in the chair.

Application

We can overcome and subdue temptation with even a little knowledge and action. We have been commanded to subdue the earth, which includes our own selves. In fact, our selves are probably the most difficult world to subdue. However, with even a little faith, we can do all things the Lord expects of us.

Scriptures

Proverbs 25:28; 1 Corinthians 9:25; Alma 38:12; Doctrine and Covenants 88:121, 123–126

Attitudes are contagious... is yours worth catching?

What Are They For?

Topics

Priesthood keys (general)

Purpose

The students will understand what is meant by "keys" and why a knowledge of how they work is essential for proper usage.

Materials

✓ A large key ring with several keys

Previous Preparation

Presentation

Hold up the set of keys and ask what they are used for. Invite a few students to come to the front and guess what specific thing any one key is used for. (The key to your house, your car, the church, an office, etc.) When it becomes apparent that it takes special knowledge (one must know which key goes into which lock) in order to use the keys, read Matthew 16:19. Jesus said that the keys of the kingdom could be used by Peter to bind (close, seal, or lock) on earth, and those same ordinances would be bound in heaven.

Application

Who holds priesthood keys today? (The President of the Church.) How are they passed on? (The President of the Church gives them to men as God designates.) Help the students understand that all ordinances performed by the priesthood power are bound for time and eternity. Priesthood power may be employed only when those who hold the keys are directed.

One of the important priesthood ordinances is temple marriage. Read Matthew 19:6 and state that when a man and woman are sealed in the temple as husband and wife, all children born to those parents are bound in a family unit for time and eternity. Only through the priesthood or through iniquity can the marriage be loosed or the seal unlocked.

Scriptures

Exodus 40:15; Matthew 16:19; Mosiah 18:18; Doctrine and Covenants 65:2

Unless you try to do something beyond what you have already mastered, you will never grow.

These Three Keys

Topics

Priesthood keys (specific)

Purpose

Students will understand that the three priesthood keys were restored to the earth by Moses, Elias and Elijah.

Materials

✓ Three large keys cut out of poster board

✓ Marker

Previous Preparation

Cut the keys out of poster board.

Presentation

Explain to the students that today they will be learning about three important priesthood keys the Lord has restored to the earth. Hold up the cut-out keys one at a time and have the students read Doctrine and Covenants 110:11–16 to find out which prophet's name should go with each of the three keys. Write the name of each prophet that restored a key on one of the cutouts. Then write on the key what each prophet restored (Moses—the keys of the gathering of Israel; Elias—the dispensation of the gospel of Abraham, or our responsibility to bless the world with the gospel; and Elijah—sacred sealing powers).

Application

Find a place in the room where you can hang the keys so that the students will remember the lesson. Discuss how each of the three keys applies to us today. (Abraham 2:8–10 offers some excellent insights into our responsibility to spread the gospel to the world.) As you talk about Elias and what he restored to the earth, reinforce the prophet's call for every worthy young man to serve a mission. Challenge the students to accept their future calls to serve.

Scriptures

Malachi 4:6; Luke 1:17; 2 Nephi 5:16; Doctrine and Covenants 2:2, 84:34, 110:11–16; Abraham 2:8–10

Sometimes success is just a matter of hanging on.

Power Connection

Topics

Priesthood power, Worthiness

Purpose

The students will better understand the source of priesthood power and that we need to be worthy to use it.

Materials

- ✓ A toaster or other electrical device that needs to be plugged into a socket
- ✓ A slice of bread

Previous Preparation

Presentation

Start off with the unplugged toaster in front of the students and tell them that you have been trying to make toast all day but haven't been able to figure out why it's not working. Place some bread in the toaster and act puzzled. Your students will easily see what is wrong and inform you that you need to plug in the toaster. Have them read Doctrine and Covenants 132:45.

Application

Just like you could not make toast because you were not plugged into the source of power, in order to use the priesthood, we must be tapped into the source of its power. It is useless unless we are plugged into its source of strength. Ask what the power source for the priesthood is. The Lord uses the priesthood, administered by mortals to bless the lives of others. All priesthood holders need to be "plugged in" just like the toaster. Even though they may go through the motions, without the proper connection to the Spirit through obedience, the priesthood power line is broken. Encourage your students to live worthily to hold and receive the blessings of the priesthood.

Scriptures

Isaiah 52:11; 2 Thessalonians 1:11; Alma 13:3; Doctrine and Covenants 132:7, 45

Diplomacy is the art of letting someone else get your way.

Is There Room?

Topics

Priorities, Time, Finances

Purpose

Students will understand that there is always room for the most important things in life if we prioritize wisely.

Materials

✓ Two clear quart jars (or similar containers)

✓ Two containers with enough marbles to fill each jar

✓ Two containers with enough grains of wheat to fill in around the marbles to fill each jar

✓ Two containers with enough water to really "fill" each jar

Previous Preparation

Presentation

Keeping the wheat and the water out of sight, fill one of the empty jars with the marbles and ask the students if the jar is full. Then add the wheat and ask if it is full now. Then add the water and ask them again if the jar is full. Explain that the marbles represent the things that we *must* do. The wheat represents things that are important for us to do. And the water represents the things we do for fun. Discuss how there is room for all.

Now pour the water from the second water container into the other empty jar, then add the wheat and next the marbles. (They will not all fit.)

Application

This demonstration will show the students that when their priorities are backwards, things don't usually work out. But when their priorities are right, everything fits nicely, whether in regards to time, money, or some other issue. (In the time example, the marbles could represent hours; the wheat could represent minutes; and the water, seconds. Other topics could also be represented.)

Scriptures

Isaiah 1:19; Luke 12:29–44; Alma 12:24; Doctrine and Covenants 72:3–4

A Hole in One

Topics

Problem solving, Thinking, Knowledge, Faith

Purpose

Students will realize that there is almost always a way to solve problems. The answers often lie within us. The Lord gave us wonderful minds that can do amazing things.

Materials

✓ Several pieces of paper (8 1/2 X 11)

✓ A pair of scissors

Previous Preparation

Learn how to cut the paper correctly by following the steps in the diagram to the right.

Presentation

Give the students the following problem to solve: show them the scissors and paper and ask how you can cut the paper so that you could make a hole large enough to climb through. Have them offer suggestions. Cut the paper in the ways they suggest, trying several ideas. When none of their suggestions work, ask if the problem really can be solved. Tell them you can do it. Ask how many believe you can do it? Why do they think you can do it? (Because you have knowledge.) Fold the paper and cut it as shown in the diagram.

Application

With knowledge we can do nearly anything. Knowledge enhances confidence. It is also important to trust the Lord because we know he has all knowledge and is able to solve any and all problems. We must learn to listen, trust and work.

Scriptures

Proverbs 3:6; Matthew 7:7; 1 Nephi 15:8; Doctrine and Covenants 9:8

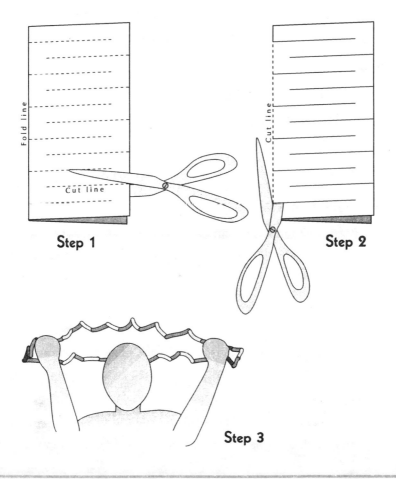

Cut line

Step 1

Cut line

Step 2

Step 3

He who throws mud loses ground.

An Inside Job

Topics

Repentance, Forgiveness, Sin

Purpose

Students will understand that through repentance, they can become clean, both inside and out. Only through repentance can we be cleansed of our sins.

Materials

- ✓ Quart jar with a lid
- ✓ Bucket of mud
- ✓ Bucket of clean water
- ✓ Hand towel

Previous Preparation

Prepare the jar by coating some of the inside with mud and screwing on the lid. Then place the jar in the bucket of mud.

Presentation

Pull out the jar from the mud and explain that the jar represents each one of us in a certain way. Ask them what they think the mud represents. (The burden we carry of the sins we commit.) What does this bucket of clean water represent? (The atonement of Christ which makes it possible for us to repent and be cleansed of our sins.) Now wash off the jar and hold it up. Are we truly clean? How do we become clean on the inside as well as the outside? Explain that the jar (or soul) has the appearance of being clean, but, in truth, it is still impure. Take off the lid and wash the jar until it is completely clean inside and out.

Application

Help students understand that repentance is not just a matter of turning away from sins in order to appear clean on the outside. True repentance is the cleansing of the inner self as well as the outer. Have each of the students relate this lesson to themselves privately by asking them the following questions: What is the mud in your life today? Are there hidden sins that need to be repented of? What steps must you take to get on the path to forgiveness? You may wish to explain the great feeling that comes from knowing that you are clean both inside and out.

Scriptures

Proverbs 28:13; Matthew 23:24–28; Mosiah 26:29; Doctrine and Covenants 19:13–21

Jumping to conclusions can be bad exercise.

No Way

Topics

Repentance, Morality, Iron rod

Purpose

Students will see that even though part of repentance is restitution, there are some things that we just cannot restore.

Materials

✓ Something breakable that can be fixed with glue

✓ Glue

✓ A raw egg

✓ A bowl

Previous Preparation

Presentation

Break the breakable item (or show two broken pieces) and have a student come up and glue them together. Discuss making mistakes and making restitution. Break the egg in the bowl and have another student come up and try to put the egg back together. Discuss why it cannot be done.

Application

Explain that some things can be forgiven but cannot be restored. (Taking someone's virtue, life, or sometimes a person's good name.) Teach them the seriousness of those mistakes we cannot mend or restore. Encourage them to stay with and value gospel principles and to keep the commandments and repent.

Scriptures

Proverbs 28:13; Luke 13:3; Alma 12:24; Doctrine and Covenants 16:6; 42:18; 76:32–35

Failure is the path of least persistence.

Don't Park in the Dark

57

Topics

Restoration of the gospel, Priesthood power

Purpose

Students will understand the importance of the restoration of the gospel and the priesthood.

Materials

✓ A flashlight

✓ Batteries for the flashlight

✓ A neon glow stick or a clock with a glowing dial

Previous Preparation

Remove the batteries from the flashlight. Set the flashlight and the glow stick on a table so all can see. Have the batteries nearby but not seen.

Presentation

Ask if the power went out and it became dark and you needed to see, which of these would you choose? (The flashlight.) Pick up the flashlight and attempt to turn it on. Ask the students what is wrong, what is needed? (Power.)

Discuss briefly the Dark Ages. Activate the glow stick. Ask what this represents. (A flicker of truth during those times.) Explain that the world needs the power of the priesthood (light and truth). Put the batteries in the flash-light and turn it on.

Application

Discuss how the gospel helps us focus on truth and knowledge. Discuss the tremendous blessing of gospel light and the fact that we do not have to be in the dark about gospel truths. Living with the light of the priesthood we see more clearly, stumble less frequently, are able to help others more often and progress more rapidly.

Scriptures

Amos 3:7; 1 Corinthians 4:20; Words of Mormon 1:17; Doctrine and Covenants 45:9

Patience is counting down without blasting off.

Ponder the List

58

Topics

Riches, Choices

Purpose

Students will see that the most important thing in life is not seeking after worldly riches but seeking after the riches of eternity.

Materials

✓ Fools gold (pyrite) or rocks painted gold

✓ Pencil and paper for each student

Previous Preparation

Presentation

Place the "gold" on a table or desk and ask what gold might represent. What things would you buy with money obtained from gold? Create a list of the things they would do with the money. Then have them look to see if any of the items are for the benefit of other people. Have them search Doctrine and Covenants 56:16–20 to find out what the Lord would think of their lists.

Application

Explain the danger of making it their priority to seek after riches in this life. Money so often leads people to stray from the Church. Ask the students why that is. What should we do to prevent this from happening to us? How can we stay focussed on the riches of eternity? What are the riches of eternity?

Scriptures

Proverbs 11:28; Jacob 2:18; Alma 1:29–30; Doctrine and Covenants 56:16–18

If you want your dreams to come true, wake up and do them.

Protection Connection

Topics

Righteousness, Angels, Divine assistance

Purpose

Students will realize that righteousness is a real form of protection.

Materials

- ✓ A sack full of wadded up pieces of paper
- ✓ A large piece of cardboard with two holes side by side in the middle for a handle like a shield

Previous Preparation

Ask three students to role play the part of "tempters" and distribute the wadded up paper among them.

Presentation

Explain that we are all in this world together, but some of us are more protected from the "world" than others. Explain that the three volunteers are from the "world" and they are constantly pelting us with temptations. Stand in the open and allow the "tempters" to throw a few "temptations" at you. Why am I hit? (Because I am unprotected.) What can I do to better protect myself? (Pray, fast, attend meetings, pay tithing, etc.) Hold up the "shield" and have the students throw a few more "temptations." What would it take to be able to call down angels from heaven for protection? (Purity of thought, charity for all, love for enemies, etc.) Ask for two volunteer "angels" to come and stand in front of you to help ward off "temptations." Call for more temptations.

Application

Are we really protected by practicing righteousness? (Yes.) Are there times when angels help us? Read together several scriptures that verify that the Lord is mindful of us and does send angels to help when we need it. Make sure they understand that one of the ways to develop righteousness is to give service—they can start by disposing of tossed "temptations."

Scriptures

Genesis 21:17; Acts 27:23; 1 Nephi 3:29; Doctrine and Covenants 27:15–18; 103:19–20

Forbidden fruit is responsible for many a bad jam.

A Sabbath Sundae

Topics

Sabbath day

Purpose

Students will recognize that Sunday is the Lord's day and that it should be kept holy.

Materials

✓ A bowl of ice cream

✓ Delicious topping for the ice cream

✓ Ketchup, mustard, and mayonnaise

Previous Preparation

Presentation

Begin by showing your students a bowl of ice cream. Ask what kinds of toppings they like on their ice cream. (Chocolate, caramel, whipped cream, etc.) Now place the delicious topping on the ice cream and ask who would like to eat some? (Most should.) Pull out your bottle of ketchup and explain that you especially love ketchup on your ice cream, as you add not only ketchup but mustard and mayonnaise to the bowl. Again ask which students would like to eat the ice cream. (None should want to now, but if one should volunteer, let him eat some.)

Application

Explain that there is nothing wrong with ketchup, mustard or mayonnaise. They are good, just not on an ice cream sundae. Ask what types of activities are not good on a Sunday? Compare the ice cream example to activities that are not good to participate in on Sundays. Also talk about the chocolate or caramel which represent activities which are appropriate on Sundays. Hold up the bowl of ice cream and ask them if this is what they are giving to the Lord on his day. Encourage them to engage in activities that keep the Lord's day holy.

Scriptures

Exodus 20:8; Luke 23:56; Doctrine and Covenants 59:9–12; Moses 3:2–3

All Things Bear Record

Topics

Savior, Symbolism

Purpose

Students will understand and remember that all things bear record of the Savior. They will remember him when they see everyday things.

Materials

✓ A rock

✓ A flower

✓ Water

✓ Picture of mountains, clouds, etc.

✓ Hymn books

Previous Preparation

Presentation

Sing "All Creatures of Our God and King" (Hymn #62). Read together Moses 6:63. Show the items and pictures of things you have selected. Ask the students how these things bear record of Christ. For example, a rock could represent the foundation of the Church, the rock of our testimonies, etc. Clouds rise from the earth (like the

Savior did) and send down shade and rain like blessings. Flowers are planted in the earth, grow up, and blossom, which could symbolize the resurrection of Christ. Christ has often been identified in the scriptures as the living water, without whom we cannot live. Soil could be compared to Christ because if we are planted in him we shall grow to our full potential.

Application

Jesus Christ created this world and is an integral part of it. Sunlight is a form of the Light of Christ. Without him, this world would not be. When we look at nature we can see that all things bear record of him. We can learn to remember the Savior when we look around us each day. When we remember him, we are more apt to keep his commandments and when we do that, we will be happier.

Scriptures

Exodus 16:4, 15; Hebrews 2:4; Alma 30:44; Moses 6:63

Minds are like parachutes—they function only when open.

Choose Your Weapon

Topics

Scriptures, Missionary work

Purpose

Students will understand that the two-edged sword spoken of in Doctrine and Covenants 12 represents the word of God, or scripture.

Materials

✓ A large sword or a picture of a two-edged sword

✓ A small 2 or 3 inch plastic sword used to hold a sandwich together

Previous Preparation

Presentation

After reading Doctrine and Covenants 12:1–2 with the students, show the large sword and compare missionary work to a battle between good and evil. Just like a warrior with a sword, we are given the word of God, or a two-edged sword, with which to battle. Next show the small toothpick-sized sword and draw a comparison between the size of the swords and the students' knowledge of the scriptures. Ask students which sword they would rather take with them into battle.

Application

This is a good exercise for students to see that they need to be studying the scriptures on a daily basis, especially those young men and women preparing to serve missions. Encourage them to study their scriptures daily to enlarge the swords they will be using in the battle for righteousness. Invite several students to share examples of how the scriptures have helped them in their lives.

Time permitting, you may want to further discuss the armor of God referred to in Ephesians 6:11–17. Verse 17 points out that the sword is the word of God and the only offensive weapon the warrior possesses. The Lord needs all the strength that we have in our missionary efforts. We need to make every effort count by putting our whole heart, might, mind, and strength into his work.

Scriptures

1 Samuel 3:1; Ephesians 6:11–17; 2 Nephi 1:26; Doctrine and Covenants 12:1–2

When looking for faults, use a mirror, not a telescope.

Sealed Tight

Topics

Sealing powers, Priesthood keys, Priesthood power, Elijah, Families

Purpose

The students will understand how important it is to become sealed as a family through proper priesthood authority.

Materials

✓ One jar of fruit (or vegetables) that is sealed—home canned or from the grocery store

✓ Another similar jar of fruit that has not been sealed and has no lid

Previous Preparation

Presentation

Show the students the two bottles of fruit and ask them what will happen to the jars in a month? a year? three years? (The sealed one will still be good to eat and the unsealed one will be spoiled.)

Application

One of the important results of the Transfiguration was the sealing power given to Peter, James, and John. Discuss the importance of this power as it relates to the jars of fruit. Bring out the idea that one is sealed and the other is not. Ask what the sealing of a fruit jar does for the fruit. Continue your questioning until someone suggests that it preserves the fruit. Now the conversation can evolve into what the sealing powers of the priesthood do for the family. Bring out the idea that many families are good and wonderful even without being sealed by the powers of the priesthood, however, their ability to remain a family in the eternities is not preserved.

Scriptures

Isaiah 22:22; Matthew 16:19; 17:1–3; Helaman 10:7; Doctrine and Covenants 68:12; 132:46

Kindness—a language the deaf can hear and the blind can see.

Obvious Choice

Topics

Serving a mission, Follow the Prophet, Choices

Purpose

Students will realize that some things the Lord asks us to do are obvious to some but not so obvious to others. We need to be wise with our stewardships.

Materials

- ✓ A screw
- ✓ Two small pieces of wood (to be screwed together)
- ✓ A screw driver
- ✓ A hammer
- ✓ A wrench
- ✓ A saw

Previous Preparation

Presentation

Explain that you have a problem: you need to fasten the two boards together with the screw. Show the several tools from which you can choose. Tell the students that the choice may seem obvious, but it may not be obvious to some. Could you fasten the two boards just using the wrench? (Possibly.) Could you do it with the hammer? (Possibly.)

Application

The Lord says that every worthy young man should serve a mission. Does serving a mission seem like an obvious choice among the choices that may be available? To some it isn't. There may be choices like marrying a high school sweetheart, a sports or music scholarship, or a lucrative job opportunity that may seem to be more important. Can a young man get by without serving a mission? (Yes.) Can you screw the two boards together with the saw? (Yes, using the edge like a screwdriver.) But to get the job done (living your life) better, there is the wise and better choice. Serving a mission can enhance growth, understanding, spirituality, and allow the Holy Ghost to expand your natural talents and abilities far beyond what you could do on your own. And there are those in the mission field who need what you have to offer. We each have a stewardship and are responsible to share the gospel.

Scriptures

Proverbs 3:13; Matthew 28:19; Alma 29:13; Doctrine and Covenants 88:81

You may not be able to direct the wind, but you can adjust your sails.

Sifting

Topics

Sifting, Follow Christ, Sermon on the Mount

Purpose

The students will understand what is meant by sifting and how it relates to them.

Materials

✓ A piece of 1/4" steel screening

✓ Some mixed gravel and sand

✓ A tray to catch the gravel and sand

Previous Preparation

Presentation

Use a screen to sift some of the gravel/sand mixture. After you have sifted it, ask the students how the Savior's sermon on the bread of life (John 6:35–71) is similar to this sifting process.

Application

The sermon separated the people who recognized Jesus as the Messiah and were willing to follow Him from the people who would not follow Him. What are some doctrines and teachings today that may separate the faithful from those who are wavering? Why did so many of Jesus' disciples leave Him? Was it that they were impressed only with the physical gifts He gave? How is it today? What about us personally? Do we go to church just to play basketball or to attend the parties, or do we go to partake of the Spirit of the Lord?

Scriptures

Amos 9:9; John 6:35–71; Alma 37:15; Doctrine and Covenants 52:12

What Signs?

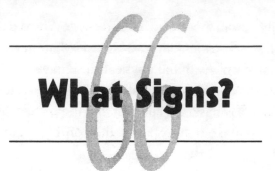

Topics

Signs, Faith, Study, Knowledge, Christ's birth, Last days

Purpose

The students will understand why it is important to know the signs of the times and to watch for them.

Materials

✓ A small, colored star

Previous Preparation

Place a small, colored star in an inconspicuous part of the room before the students arrive. Be sure it is placed so everyone can see it.

Presentation

Do not make reference to the star until after the lesson is started. Tell the students that without looking around, they should write down the color of the star in the room. Ask why some have forgotten the color. Ask if the wise men were the only ones who saw the star at the birth of Jesus. It's likely that many on the earth could have noticed it but probably did not understand its significance. The wise men knew about the star because they had faithfully studied the prophecies in the scriptures.

Application

Ask what lesson of life can be learned from this. Signs are all around us, but we need to know what to look for and to be spiritually alert to promptings that may come. When we are sensitive to the spirit, we will hear answers to our questions and will hear the Lord's promptings because we have been listening. We will see eternal relationships and prophesies come true because we have been watching. To those who are spiritually sensitive, prepared, and responsive, signs and occurrences that seem meaningless to others will often appear to them as manifestations or symbols of divine importance.

Scriptures

Isaiah 7:14; Matthew 2:1–23; 3 Nephi 1:21; Doctrine and Covenants 29:14

Feed your faith and doubt will starve to death.

Even Tied

Topics

Sin, Disobedience, Foolishness, Freedom

Purpose

Students will realize that sin restricts our choices and is foolish.

Materials

✓ Rope

✓ A cloth to protect the wrists

Previous Preparation

Presentation

Ask for two volunteers. Have one tie the other's hands with the rope (over the cloth so as not to cause injury or pain). What are things the tied up student can't do in this condition? What are things that can tie us up spiritually? What do they prevent us from doing or becoming?

Application

When we sin, we restrict our freedom (freedom to feel worthy, freedom to feel happy, etc. . . .). Satan's desire is to bind us and lead us down to hell. He can only do this if we let him. Encourage the students to be wise and stay away from activities that will tie them up; don't play with the "ropes" of evil.

Scriptures

Isaiah 52:1–3; Matthew 22:1–13; 2 Nephi 1:13; Moses 7:26

Keep Looking

68

Topics

Spirit

Purpose

Students will understand that when we look for the Spirit we can find it.

Materials

✓ Two different air freshener cans

Previous Preparation

Presentation

Have all the students put their heads down and close their eyes. Spray one scent in one part of the room and have the students raise their hands as soon as they smell the scent in the air. Spray a different scent in another part of the room and have the students do the same thing again. How many of you were searching for the smell? Did it take some longer than others to smell the scent? Not everyone feels the Spirit at the same time. Would you have noticed the scent had you not been seeking for it so intently? (You could also spray a little scent in the room before class and see how many noticed it when they came in.) Do you look for the Spirit in the same way that you were looking for the scent? Why is it important to attend class, go to church, etc. expecting to feel the Spirit?

Application

This is a good lesson to show the students that they need to do their part in seeking the Spirit.

Scriptures

1 Chronicles 28:9; Hebrews 9:28; 1 Nephi 10:19; Doctrine and Covenants 88:63

He Is Talking to You

69

Topics

Spirit, Listening

Purpose

The students will be able to recognize what the Spirit is like.

Materials

- ✓ About 10 different objects that can be dropped on a desk without breaking
- ✓ A cover so the objects cannot be seen
- ✓ Paper and pencil for each person

Previous Preparation

Presentation

Without letting the students see any of the objects, drop each one on the desk and tell what each object is as you drop it. Next, randomly drop the objects as students write down what they think they are. How closely did you have to listen to find out what the objects were? Do you listen that closely to the Spirit? How can we benefit from listening to the Spirit? Why is it important to understand how the Spirit works?

Application

Not everyone feels the Spirit in the same way, so it is important that we know when it is working with us. The closer that we listen for the Spirit, the more we are able to hear it. We need to be in tune with the Spirit to know what it is saying. This initial discussion can lead to a discussion of what we need to do to have the Spirit with us in our lives.

Scriptures

Nehemiah 9:20; 1 Corinthians 2:10; Helaman 5:29–30; Doctrine and Covenants 88:66

There is no right way to do a wrong thing.

We Are Alike

Topics

Spirit body

Purpose

Students will learn that their spirits and their physical bodies are alike in appearance.

Materials

✓ A skin-tight surgical glove

Previous Preparation

Presentation

Show students the surgical glove, then place it on your hand. Point out how the glove conforms to your hand and how they become similar in size and shape. You may also want to have a student come to the front and put on the glove, demonstrating the fact that the glove assumes the shape of any hand.

Application

Explain that the hand represents the physical body and the glove represents the spirit. Discuss the relationship between the spirit and the body and what they have in common. They both are material, however the spirit is more refined and elastic and can exist outside of the physical body as well as inside a body of any shape.

Scriptures

Psalms 82:6; Ether 3:16–17; Doctrine and Covenants 77:2; Abraham 3:22–26

Of all the things you wear, your expression is the most important.

Measuring Up

Topics

Spirituality, Judging, Pre-mortal world

Purpose

Students will think about their own spiritual "height." Students will learn to have their own measuring stick and not judge others.

Materials

✓ Two different looking tape measures

✓ A chair to stand on

Previous Preparation

Presentation

Invite several students to come forward. With one of the tape measures (the other is not visible to the students) measure the height of the students. Explain that you have just measured their physical heights. Have them take their seats. But what about their spiritual heights? What if we had a special instrument to measure one's spirituality? Pull out the other tape measure. Invite another student to come up (one who you know keeps the commandments). Explain that every commandment lived faithfully measures about a foot on the "spirit-o-meter." Ask the student questions like "do you pray sincerely?" "do you pay tithing out of love?" "do you ponder the scriptures?" etc. Measure up a foot with each yes answer. Ask enough questions so that you have to stand on a chair to keep measuring.

Application

How spiritually "tall" are you? Discuss how "tall" they may have been in their pre-mortal lives and what it takes to "measure up" to the Lord's expectations here in mortality. Also bring up the fact that we cannot judge a person's true spirituality by outward measures, but only by their hearts. Discuss the fact that there are some people who pray, read scriptures, and pay tithing who are not very spiritual in their hearts. The Lord knows our hearts. He knows if we are striving or not. He knows how tall we are. Judgement should be left to him. We should spend our effort in developing our own spirituality and not comparing ourselves to others.

Scriptures

1 Samuel 16:7; Mosiah 29:12; Doctrine and Covenants 1:10; Abraham 3:22–23

There are many questions no man can answer... and most of them are asked by 5-year-olds.

Take a Stand

Topics

Stand in holy places, Sin

Purpose

Students will realize the importance of staying away from sin by standing in holy places.

Materials

✓ A three to six foot length of string

✓ A heavy item to tie to the string (like a stapler)

Previous Preparation

Tie the heavy item to the string and attach the other end of string to the ceiling or light fixture so that the heavy object is hanging down about two feet off the floor.

Presentation

Invite a student to come to the front and stand a few feet away from the hanging object. Pull the object close to his nose, tell him to stand very still, then let go. On the return swing it will come close but not hit his nose (due to gravity and air friction). Ask the students what would have happened if the student stepped forward or even leaned his head in that direction just a little. (It would have hit his nose.)

Application

If the object represents sin, what does it mean to "stand in holy places"? Help the students understand that when they are living the gospel they are standing in holy places and sin won't tempt them. However, sometimes if they even turn just a little toward sin, it will smack them and hurt them. Explain that it is best to move away from sin and not tempt it or flirt with it.

Scriptures

2 Chronicles 35:5; 1 Corinthians 3:16–17; 2 Nephi 9:45; Doctrine and Covenants 45:32

Burdens should never get us down, except on our knees to pray.

Get a Grip

Topics

Strength of the Lord, Dependence on the Lord, Arm of flesh, Trust in the Lord

Purpose

Students will understand that they need to learn to rely on the Lord for strength. This activity will help students see that their own strength often fails them, while the Lord's strength is enduring.

Materials

✓ Two-handled spring hand grip

✓ A penny

✓ A stopwatch or clock

Previous Preparation

Presentation

Tell the students that you want to conduct a little contest to see who is the strongest. All you have to do is hold the hand grip closed tight enough to hold the penny in place between the handles. With a stop watch or by watching the clock, you will discover which student holds the penny in place for the longest amount of time. (You may wish to declare both a boy and a girl winner.

Most students will not be able to hold the penny in place for much more than a minute or so.

Application

Students will see that although they may have great strength, it may not be enduring. Point out that at first it is fairly easy for them to hold the hand grip closed. As time moves on, it becomes more difficult until eventually they lose their strength and falter. This is one of the ways Satan works. He lets you think you can do things without the Lord's help by making it seem easy at first. Thought-provoking questions could include: What can you do to rely more on the Lord? How would relying on the Lord fortify you to overcome some of the "grippers" in your life?

Scriptures

Isaiah 40:31; 2 Corinthians 12:9; 1 Nephi 10:6; Doctrine and Covenants 3:4

Life is like a tennis game—you can't win without serving.

Give Them a Hand

Topics

Temple work, Family history, Love of others, Families, Elijah

Purpose

Students will realize the importance of temple work for those on the other side of the veil.

Materials

Previous Preparation

Presentation

Have one student stand at one end of the room. Have another student stand at the opposite end of the room. Explain to the class that they must tie, link, connect, or bind these two students together, but the students are not allowed to move. Ask the class to solve the problem. (If nothing happens, ask one or two outgoing students to link the students together, hoping they will start the human chain by taking the hands of the students at the ends of the room). Keep asking students to join in until the students at the ends of the room are linked together.

Application

How can we link a person standing here on earth to a person standing on the other side of the veil? (Temple work.) Discuss the importance of each one of us doing our part. We are an important link to our ancestors. Others depend on us; they cannot do it by themselves or for themselves. The Lord has commanded us to do this work.

Scriptures

Malachi 4:5–6; 1 Corinthians 15:29; Helaman 10:7; Doctrine and Covenants 2:2

People who do things that count never stop to count them.

On the Rocks

Topics

Testimony, Faith, Integrity, Three degrees of glory

Purpose

Students will understand the importance of having strong testimonies.

Materials

- ✓ A grain of sand
- ✓ A gravel-sized pebble
- ✓ A marble-sized pebble
- ✓ A small rock
- ✓ A large rock

Previous Preparation

Presentation

Place the grain of sand on the table or desk. Invite a person to come up and, from some distance away, blow it off the table. Place the gravel on the table and have another person come blow it away. Next place the marble-sized pebble and have another come and try. Now place the small rock and have another person come and try to blow it off the table. Finally, place the large rock and do the same. You may wish to have several people come up at once and try to blow the large rock off the table.

Application

In this demonstration, who did the volunteers represent? (Satan, the world, evil people or influences.) Who did the sand represent? (Maybe the sons of perdition, those totally past feeling.) Ask the same question for each of the rocks. Gravel could represent evil people, those who hate the Lord, telestial; the marble could represent terrestrial people, those who come to church but not accept callings, etc.; the small rock could represent people on the road to being celestial candidates, those who are really trying and building their faith; the large rock could represent those who have celestial perspective, firm faith, those who are obedient, etc.

Scriptures

1 Chronicles 19:13; Luke 8:5–8; Alma 37:15; Doctrine and Covenants 76:43–86

Start doing today what you wish to do well tomorrow.

Don't Be Blown Away

Topics

Testimony, Temptations, Follow the Prophet, Gospel

Purpose

Students will realize the importance of strong testimonies in the gospel, Christ, and the prophets.

Materials

- ✓ A feather
- ✓ A large rock

Previous Preparation

Presentation

Place the feather on a table and ask a student to come and blow the feather off the table. Place the rock on the table and have another student come and try to blow it off the table. You may want to have several students together try to blow the rock off the table.

Application

We must be strong. Our testimonies must be firm, solid, and built on the rock of revelation. Our foundation must be the Savior and we must believe in and follow the prophet of God. If we have this foundation, we will not be blown away by temptations.

Scriptures

Psalms 18:2; Ephesians 4:14; 3 Nephi 14:24–25; Doctrine and Covenants 8:2–3

Children have never been very good at listening to their elders, but they have never failed to imitate them.

Think

Topics

Thinking, Gift of our minds, Faith, Problem solving, Knowledge

Purpose

Students will appreciate the gift of their minds and start to look beyond average thinking patterns. They will be able to solve problems more effectively.

Materials

- ✓ A chalk board or poster board
- ✓ A piece of chalk or marker
- ✓ Paper and pencil for each student

Previous Preparation

Draw on the chalkboard or poster board figures A and B.

Presentation

Refer to figure A and ask the students how many squares they see. (Most will see sixteen, but some will see seventeen—sixteen small ones and one around the outside.) Discuss why some students see sixteen and others see more. Others will then probably see four more, four blocks of four in each corner, then they will see even more. (There are 30 total.)

Next have the students draw figure B on a piece of paper. Tell them to connect all nine dots using only four straight lines without picking up their pencils and without going through any dot more than once. Figure C shows one solution if you draw the lines in order, 1 through 4.

Application

Discuss the importance of thinking creatively. By learning to utilize our minds more effectively, we can do more, be more, serve more. Discuss the mind as a gift from the Lord. Explain that we have to get out of our "mental boxes"—go beyond inhibited thinking. Remind them that prayer is an excellent way to "go beyond ourselves."

Scriptures

Isaiah 26:3; 2 Timothy 1:7; Alma 32:34; Doctrine and Covenants 9:8; 84:85

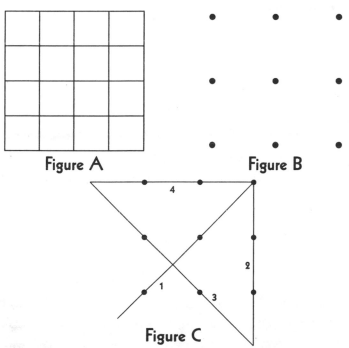

Figure A   Figure B

Figure C

The SWAT Team

Topics

Thoughts, Self-discipline

Purpose

Students will realize the importance of clean and good thoughts.

Materials

✓ A fly swatter

Previous Preparation

Presentation

Show the fly swatter and ask the class what it is. What is it for? (Killing flies.) What other insects can we swat? Why do we use fly swatters? (To keep our homes cleaner and to be free from annoying insects.) What are things in our spiritual lives we can and should swat? Read Mosiah 4:30.

Application

If we allow flies to fly freely in our homes, what could happen? (They would lay eggs, there would be more flies, more disease.) What happens if we let our thoughts fly freely without watching them? What kind of thoughts should we swat? (Negative, immoral, angry, vengeful, mean, etc.) Discuss ways to keep our thoughts positive, moral, kind, etc.

Scriptures

Isaiah 55:7; Matthew 15:17–20; Mosiah 4:30; Doctrine and Covenants 88:69

A ship is safe in the harbor, but that isn't what ships were built for.

A Plead to Read

Topics

Time, Scriptures, Stewardship

Purpose

Students will understand that in an eternal perspective it is more important to spend quality time reading the scriptures as opposed to always being involved in other, less worthwhile activities like watching TV.

Materials

✓ A set of scriptures

✓ Several church books with which students would be familiar

Previous Preparation

Presentation

Bring out all the books you have collected and hold them up one by one. Take a moment to discuss what each one means to you and what you have learned by reading the books. By the end, you should have a stack of books a couple of feet high. Then share the following excerpt with your students:

"If you have a twenty-hour-a-week television habit and would repent and convert it into a gospel study habit, in one year you could read The Book of Mormon, The Doctrine and Covenants, The Pearl of Great Price, and the entire Bible. In addition, you could read Jesus the Christ, The Articles of Faith, Gospel Principles, the basic priesthood manual, the basic woman's manual, the basic children's manual, all three volumes of Doctrines of Salvation, The Miracle of Forgiveness, The Promised Messiah, Essentials in Church History, and could then reread the Bible, Book of Mormon, Doctrine and Covenants, and Pearl of Great Price. This would still leave time to read the Ensign, The New Era, and The Friend each month and the Church News each week. This is based on your ability to read only ten pages an hour."

Elder William R. Bradford, Oct. 1979 Conference Report

Application

Challenge your students to read daily from the scriptures and reap the promised blessings.

Scriptures

Proverbs 1:5; John 5:39; Jacob 4:6; 7:23; Doctrine and Covenants 11:22; 26:1; 88:118

The secret to life is not to do what you like, but to like what you do.

It's About Time

80

Topics

Time, Stewardship, Agency

Purpose

Students will learn to make time more meaningful and to use it wisely.

Materials

- ✓ A clock
- ✓ A tool
- ✓ A spoon
- ✓ A pillow
- ✓ A book
- ✓ A video cassette

Previous Preparation

Presentation

Show the clock and explain that it represents time. (Time in school, time together as a family, time on earth, etc.) Show the other items separately and ask the students what they think these objects might represent in relation to time. (Pillow=sleeping time, book=study time, video=time for entertainment, spoon=eating time, tool=work time, serving others.)

Application

Discuss the value of time. Explain that we have all the time there is—24 hours a day—but it is how we use it that creates success or failure, joy or sadness, happiness or misery. It is up to us. We really are in charge of our time, whether we think so or not. Encourage the students to look at how they use this valuable gift of time and see if there are areas that could be better prioritized.

Scriptures

Ecclesiastes 3:1–8; Romans 13:11; Alma 12:24; Doctrine and Covenants 60:13

There is one redeeming thing about a mistake—it proves that somebody stopped talking long enough to do something.

Walls

Topics

Time, Temptations

Purpose

Students will realize that the places they spend their time greatly influence what they do and become. It is much easier to resist the temptation to drink, smoke, or any other temptation if we distance ourselves from those situations. This lesson is ideal for those students who think they can always avoid temptation no matter where they go.

Materials

✓ A candy bar

Previous Preparation

Presentation

Begin by telling the students you are going to give a candy bar to whoever can bend over and pick it up. But there are some rules: they must keep their legs straight and not bend their knees and they must also bend down straight forward. Explain that you want them all to practice before you choose a few to try for the candy bar. Have them stand and bend over to touch the floor. Most will be able to, which will bolster their hopes of receiving the candy bar. Now pick four or five students to come to the front. This time have them stand against the wall with their heels touching the baseboard. Inform them that the candy bar is theirs if they can pick it up without bending their knees or falling forward. They must remain standing. (No one will be able to it because the wall prevents them from bending all the way down.)

Application

Describe how some things are easy to do when the situation is right. But when the situation is altered, the task becomes more difficult. Ask what the wall represents? (Temptations.) What are some of the walls you are facing in life? How can you overcome them? Allow the students to draw as many conclusions as they can from their own experiences.

Scriptures

Proverbs 1:10; 1 Corinthians 10:13; 1 Nephi 15:24; Doctrine and Covenants 87:8

When there's work to be done, turn up your sleeves, not your nose.

Give It Back

Topics

Tithing, Faith

Purpose

Students will better understand the principle of tithing and be committed to live it.

Materials

- ✓ Ten pennies
- ✓ Ten dimes
- ✓ Ten dollar bills
- ✓ Ten ten dollar bills
- ✓ Ten one hundred-dollar bills (real or play money)

Previous Preparation

Presentation

Hand a student ten pennies. Ask him to give one back to you. Do you mind giving back just a penny? Hand another student ten dimes and ask for one back. Is it difficult to give up a dime? Give another student ten $1 bills and ask for one back. What could you buy with a dollar? Is it difficult to give it back? Give another student ten $10 bills and ask the same questions. Then hand a student ten $100 bills and ask for one back. Discuss the fact that it is a little harder to give back the amounts that are worth more.

Application

Explain that tithing is not a money principle, but a faith principle. The Lord wants our faith, not really our money. Discuss the principle that paying a penny tithing or $1000 tithing really is the same if it is a full tithing. Paying tithing helps us to be unselfish and learn to live the law of consecration.

Scriptures

Deuteronomy 12:6; Luke 16:10; 3 Nephi 24:10; Doctrine and Covenants 1:17, 21

Change is often desirable, frequently necessary, and always inevitable.

Not Quite

Topics

Tithing, Faith, Obedience

Purpose

Students will feel the importance of being full-tithe payers.

Materials

- ✓ Ten cookies
- ✓ A sign that reads "BISHOP"
- ✓ A chalkboard or poster board
- ✓ A piece of chalk or marker

Previous Preparation

Presentation

Place the cookies in a row on the table or desk and explain that these represent your income for the month. Take away two cookies to "pay for" your mortgage payment, one cookie for food, one cookie for clothing, one cookie for utilities, two cookies for a car payment, one for a credit card loan, and one for insurance, so there is only one left. Have a volunteer come up and place the "bishop" sign around his neck. Explain to the "bishop" that it has been a difficult month and you still have other bills to pay. Tell the "bishop" that you are sure the Lord will understand if you pay only a partial tithing this month. Then take a big bite of the cookie and hand it to the "bishop."

Application

Write the word TITHING on the chalkboard. Ask what a part tithing is called. (Erase the TI—it is just a *thing*.) Discuss the principle of tithing and being faithful. Be sure they understand that tithing is not a money principle; it is a faith principle.

Scriptures

1 Samuel 15:22; Malachi 3:8; Alma 13:15; Doctrine and Covenants 119

Most parents are convinced that if their children have talent, 'it's inherited; but if they have any meanness, it's picked up from the neighbor kids.

Soil for the Soul

Topics

Trust in the Lord, Trust in the prophet, Obedience

Purpose

Students will learn to put their trust in the Lord and the Prophets, even when it may seem illogical to do so.

Materials

- ✓ Dark cookie crumbs
- ✓ Small, clear container
- ✓ Seeds
- ✓ A spoon

Previous Preparation

Place the dark cookie crumbs in the container. (This is to appear like soil.)

Presentation

Display the container of "soil" and the seeds on a table or desk. Make a hole in the middle of the crumbs with the spoon and ask a student to come up and plant a seed in the rich "potting soil." While he is doing this, briefly discuss how things grow. Before the student sits back down, ask him to take a spoonful of the "soil" and eat it. Assure him it will not hurt him, that he will like it. If he refuses, invite a willing volunteer.

Application

Discuss the principle of trusting in the Lord and His Prophets, even when it seems illogical to do so. Why can we trust God? (He has all knowledge and all love for us.) Discuss examples in the students' lives where they trusted in the Lord, the Prophet, or parents.

Scriptures

Proverbs 29:25; Hebrews 2:13; Alma 5:13; Doctrine and Covenants 11:12

One thing you can't recycle is wasted time.

Cut Through

85

Topics

Truth, Scriptures, Missionary work

Purpose

Students will understand that truth will cut through ignorance, confusion, and worldly wisdom.

Materials

- ✓ A toilet paper roll tube
- ✓ A treat that can be cut in two and will fit in the tube
- ✓ Old or old looking, unappealing paper
- ✓ A sharp kitchen knife with a serrated edge

Previous Preparation

Put the treat inside the tube and then wrap the tube in the unappealing paper.

Presentation

Show the wrapped tube and ask what they think is inside. Do they think they know what is inside? Ask if it is worth finding out. How can they know? Invite two volunteers to help find out what is inside. Have each hold an end of the package. Cut through the wrapping, tube, and treat. Remove the two halves of the treat and give to your helpers. Was it worth finding out? Spiritually speaking, what do the parts of the demonstration represent? Treat? (Blessings, joy, gospel, etc.) Outer wrapper and the tube? (Ignorance, world's wisdom misunderstanding, confusion) Knife? (Truth, scriptures, prophets, Holy Ghost, gospel knowledge, missionaries, etc.)

Application

We can cut through the ignorance of the world with truth, the Lord's wisdom, His word, and the words of His prophets. We have the truth and it is delicious to the soul, wonderful, and worth the effort.

Scriptures

Psalms 51:6; Ephesians 4:18; Moroni 10:4; Doctrine and Covenants 6:7

Swallowing your pride seldom leads to indigestion.

Stick Together

Topics

Unity, Friends

Purpose

The students will better understand that each person is unique, with unique strengths and weaknesses. They will understand that by themselves they may be weak, but together they are strong.

Materials

✓ A small stick or tree branch for each person (have extra)

✓ A ball of string

Previous Preparation

Presentation

Place the sticks on the table and ask the students to come and choose a stick that matches their personality. Once they have chosen their sticks, ask several students why they chose the sticks they did and how they are different from the others. What are the differences, the similarities? Are some sticks stronger? What makes them stronger than the others? Does someone have a stick that you cannot break? (Do not try.) Now gather up all the sticks into a bundle and tie them with the string. Can you break the sticks now?

Application

How are people different? How are they alike? How are sticks, in this instance, like people? What is the result of people coming together and helping each other? Encourage the students to "stick together," be true friends, and serve each other.

Scriptures

Proverbs 18:24; John 17:21; Mosiah 18:21; Doctrine and Covenants 88:133

Hug your kids at home—belt them in the car.

The Weak Will Rule

Topics

Weak things become strong, Humility, Judging

Purpose

Students will realize what the Lord means when He talks about His obedient children as the weak things of the world. They will be encouraged to always seek to have the Lord on their side.

Materials

✓ A wooden yardstick (or similar board) that you do not mind breaking

✓ Newspaper

Previous Preparation

Practice the demonstration.

Presentation

Show the yardstick and the sheet of newspaper. Which is the stronger? (Most will say the yardstick.) If you had to defend yourself, which would you choose? (Again, most will choose the yardstick.) Place the yardstick on the edge of a table so that almost one half of the stick hangs over the edge. Cover the part of the yardstick on the table with one sheet of newspaper, flattened out on the table. Ask what will happen if the yardstick is hit.

(Most will say the paper will fly up.) Go ahead and hit the stick hard. It should break. (The reason is there is a large column of air pushing on the surface of the newspaper—air pressure. If the paper is moved too quickly, the surrounding air does not have time to flow under the paper to equalize the pressure. Trying to lift the paper is like trying to lift several tons with the tiny stick.)

Application

Explain that the paper represents us, the weak things of the world. But when we have learned to prostrate ourselves before the Lord in humility and call upon unseen forces to help us solve our problems or contend with our enemies, he strengthens us.

Scriptures

Isaiah 40:31; Matthew 23:12; Ether 12:27; Doctrine and Covenants 1:28

The happiness of your life depends on the quality of your thoughts.

Arise and Be Wise

Topics

Word of Wisdom, Choices

Purpose

Students will understand that their bodies truly are temples and they should act accordingly.

Materials

- ✓ A delicate potted flower
- ✓ A clear glass of paint thinner, marked
- ✓ A clear glass of water, marked
- ✓ A shiny shoe
- ✓ A file
- ✓ A soft cloth
- ✓ An electric tool
- ✓ A small vial of oil, marked
- ✓ A small vial of sand, marked
- ✓ A slice of bread
- ✓ A jar of peanut butter, marked
- ✓ A jar of mud, marked
- ✓ A picture of a temple

Previous Preparation

Prepare the above items.

Presentation

Show the flower and two glasses of liquid and ask which the students would use to nourish the plant? Show the tool, oil, and sand and ask which they would use to lubricate the tool? Show the shoe, cloth, and file and ask which they would use to polish the shoe? Show the bread, peanut butter, and mud and ask which they would use to make a sandwich. Show the picture of the temple and ask which they would wear inside—clean, white clothing or stained and dirty work clothes. Now ask, what about your bodies? How does this discussion relate to you and your bodies?

Application

Discuss the fact that our Father in Heaven has told us that our bodies are truly temples of our spirits. How should we treat them? How should we treat someone else's body? What kinds of things should and shouldn't we be taking inside our bodies?

Scriptures

Proverbs 3:13; James 1:5; Alma 37:35; Doctrine and Covenants 89

Break a bad habit—drop it.

Appendix

The following pages are blank lesson forms that you can use to write down your own ideas for object lessons.

Use any ideas that come to you. Feel free to write in the book. Use this book as a tool.

Also, if you would like to be a part of Volume 2, please submit your object lesson ideas—your own originals or others—along with your name, address and telephone number. If selected, you will be credited for submitting the idea.

Title:

Topics

Purpose

Materials

Previous Preparation

Presentation

Application

Scriptures

Title:

Topics

Purpose

Materials

Previous Preparation

Presentation

Application

Scriptures

5

Title:

Topics

Purpose

Materials

Previous Preparation

Presentation

Application

Scriptures

7

Title:

Topics

Purpose

Materials

Previous Preparation

Presentation

Application

Scriptures

Title:

Topics

Purpose

Materials

Previous Preparation

Presentation

Application

Scriptures

Title:

Topics

Purpose

Materials

Previous Preparation

Presentation

Application

Scriptures

Title:

Topics

Purpose

Materials

Previous Preparation

Presentation

Application

Scriptures

Title:

Topics

Purpose

Materials

Previous Preparation

Presentation

Application

Scriptures

Title:

Topics

Purpose

Materials

Previous Preparation

Presentation

Application

Scriptures

Title:

Topics

Purpose

Materials

Previous Preparation

Presentation

Application

Scriptures

Topic Index

24

Object Index